Dyslexia in the Digital Age

Also available from Continuum

100 Ideas for Supporting Pupils with Dyslexia, Gavin Reid and
  Shannon Green

Dyslexia 2nd Edition, Gavin Reid

Meeting the Needs of Students with Dyslexia, June Massey

Supporting Children with Dyslexia 2nd Edition, Garry Squires and Sally
  McKeown

The Teaching Assistant's Guide to Dyslexia, Gavin Reid and Shannon
  Green

Dyslexia in the Digital Age

Making IT Work

Ian Smythe

Resources to accompany this book are available online at: http://education.smythe.continuumbooks.com

Please visit the link and register with us to receive your password and to access these downloadable resources.

If you experience any problems accessing the resources, please contact Continuum at: info@continuumbooks.com

continuum

Continuum International Publishing Group

The Tower Building
11 York Road
London
SE1 7NX

80 Maiden Lane, Suite 704
New York, NY 10038

www.continuumbooks.com
http://education.smythe.continuumbooks.com

© Ian Smythe 2010

British Library Cataloguing-in-Publication Data
A catalogue record for this book is available from the British Library.

ISBN: 9780826438836 (paperback)
9780826430823 (hardcover)

Library of Congress Cataloging-in-Publication Data
A catalogue record for this book has been applied for from the Library of Congress

Typeset by Ben Cracknell Studios

Printed and bound in Great Britain by Bell & Bain Ltd, Glasgow

Contents

Preface   vii

Acknowledgements   xi

1 Definition of Dyslexia   1

2 Testing   13

3 Assistive Hardware   37

4 Assistive Software   67

5 Literacy Learning Software   99

6 The User Interface   115

7 E-learning and Knowledge Assessment   139

8 Multilingualism   165

9 Conclusion: Spreading the Word   183

References   191

Index   196

Preface

Health warning – if you want to get stuck into the technology and not worry about definition and assessment, you may like to jump straight to Chapter 3. But if you would like the contexts it is recommended you start at the beginning.

When you flick through this book, your first question will probably be 'But where are all the illustrations?' After not very much deliberation, we decided to omit pictures because it was obvious that it would make the book look out of date very quickly. In particular, if I said that such-and-such a piece of software had x failing, the software manufacturers would change it immediately, thereby undermining the integrity of the book.

We then thought, 'If we list names of software, that too could quickly become out of date. So let's put them on a website.' Good idea. But then I decided that I still wanted a book that I would want to buy. That is, I would like to see some of the software that has informed the ideas behind this book. Yes, the fact that you are reading this book suggests that you have a computer, broadband and an interest in the subject. Therefore, you should not be worried about having to refer to an online webpage. But, at the same time, if I were reading it on the train, I would want to get out my highlighter and mark anything that might be of interest, particularly when I do not know about it. For this reason, we have produced what may be described as a compromise with respect to the subject of the book and the needs of the diverse readers.

In addition to this book, you can also access the dedicated Continuum website which will have links to software mentioned in this book. This will be periodically reviewed and updated. Furthermore, you can also look for the latest information, news and software on my own website (www.ibisconsultants.info) and on my blog (http://technodys.blogspot.com) which is updated daily.

About the book – why it exists

This book is about the role of technology in the lives of dyslexic individuals, whether they are in primary school, at university, at work or any other place. The technology has become so ubiquitous that we tend to forget it. Most of the time it is enabling, although sometimes it can add to life's hassles. People offer technology as a panacea for dyslexia, but rarely has anybody stood back and properly addressed such fundamental questions as:

1. What technology already exists to help dyslexic individuals?
2. How can that help with respect to the specific difficulties of a given dyslexic individual?
3. How useful is it and how do you prove it?
4. How will the user learn how to use it?
5. If there are two pieces of software with similar capabilities, how do we know which is better?
6. When should they switch to something else?
7. Why spend a lot of money on software when so much of it is free?

And many, many more questions!

This book is designed to offer guidance to the technology and show how it can support the dyslexic individual, and answer these questions. It does not attempt to make specific recommendations since, as mentioned above, the speed of change in terms of both the hardware and the software means that whatever is talked about now may be obsolete in a year and any shortcomings could be modified within weeks of publication. Any competitive edge could be lost overnight as changes are made as a consequence of highlighting differences. Instead the focus here is on the concepts and the 'theory', which should allow people to make informed choices, but with information designed to help find solutions.

We tried to come up with a list of who would be interested in this book. The list included dyslexia assessors, ICT assessors, MSc students, university disability officers, university tutors, university dyslexia support workers, HR in businesses, disability officers in businesses, teachers/SENCOs, ICT specifiers in LEAs, e-learning developers, software developers, website developers, technology lecturers, those teaching dyslexic individuals in schools, those supporting dyslexics at home, assistive technology suppliers and dyslexic individuals. Of course not all chapters will be of interest to everybody. So pick and choose to your heart's content!

Guide to the chapters

The starting point for this book has to be one of setting the scene. That is, providing a clear understanding of what dyslexia is. However, it might seem more reasonable to leave that to another book and just cross-refer to it, focusing solely here on the technology. But what would that other text have to cover? At the very least it would have to bring in the latest arguments, the logic behind types of assessment, the models of evaluation and support as well as the roles and responsibilities of those involved. And provide all this in such a way that it could be linked to the technology described in this book. Sadly no such other text exists. So this book starts by defining dyslexia. Only then can we begin to understand what is needed to develop appropriate support, this is found in Chapter 1.

The rest of this book is dedicated to the technology and how it can be used. However, it would be easy to fall into the trap of many other books, and create a tome that is already out of date before it hits the shelves, because the product has already changed or no longer exists. One of the guiding principles behind this book is not only to provide what is current, but to present it in a theoretical as well as a practical manner, so that the book's usefulness will last beyond that of any specific technology.

There are two main areas for testing with respect to the dyslexic individual – testing of skills and abilities, and the testing of knowledge. Chapter 2 is concerned with skills testing, particularly regarding the underlying characteristics of the difficulties of a dyslexic individual. This includes literacy and underlying cognitive difficulties. Furthermore, related areas such as study skills are also considered.

Chapter 3 concentrates on the assistive hardware that currently exists to help the dyslexic individual. The chapter looks at generic and specialist hardware as well as providing an overview of the main components that will allow informed choices to be made.

The chapter on assistive software, Chapter 4, analyses both text-to-speech and speech-to-text technology, looking at the diversity of formats available and their implications, and discusses concept mapping. However, there are many other types of software that can assist the dyslexic individual.

Education has many facets, but a key area is the acquisition of both literacy skills and knowledge. Chapter 5 presents software with respect to the defining characteristic of dyslexic individuals:

literacy acquisition. This chapter looks at the different skills that can be taught, and the research to back up the claims of technology, as well as discussing the independence of the research.

Chapter 6 attempts to pull together the diverse strands that impact upon the user interface. The issues addressed are usability, including interface design (and the ability to adjust to the user's preferences) and readability, as well as the need to ensure content can be used in conjunction with text-to-speech and other accessibility software.

E-learning and technology-led knowledge assessments are predicted to be pervasive in education, with technologists trying to throw new tools at it while educators try to come to grips with the new pedagogy. Chapter 7 attempts to provide a background to the implications of e-learning for dyslexic individuals.

With an estimated 10 per cent of the UK population currently using more than one language, multilingualism is now an important issue. Chapter 8 looks at this in relation to dyslexia and how technology can play a key role in the support of these individuals, whether they are Welsh first language speakers, Chinese speakers in Manchester or Bulgarian dyslexic students in London.

Technology is moving fast, as is the desire to implement change, especially before there are too many court cases over discrimination against dyslexic individuals. The final chapter, Chapter 9, attempts to delineate what have been the barriers to progress to date, and how change will happen, due to legislation, technology and the desire for change, and makes a tentative prediction of the future.

Web 1.0, 2.0 and 3.0

There is much confusion over the terminology of Web 1.0, Web 2.0 and Web 3.0. They may be regarded as a simple linguistic device to demonstrate progress from a simple, fairly passive system of Web 1.0 the content of which was delivered by a small group of people, to an interactive, participatory web in Web 2.0. The principle of Web 3.0 is that greater use is made of the material of others, creating a form of semantic interaction, and is sometimes referred to as the Semantic Web. However, some people, such as the inventor of the world wide web, Sir Tim Berners-Lee, would suggest these are terms without meaning since there is no real distinction between each, and the functionality some refer to as Web 2.0 was around long before the term was coined.

Acknowledgements

This is the culmination of talking to thousands of people over many years and across many continents. And, like most authors, I would like to acknowledge their contributions, the big ones and the small ones, but life is too short. So I shall restrict it to those I consider to have made the most significant contributions – Holly Myers, Vivian Ward and Susan Dunsmore.

And not forgetting a whole host of friends around the world.

1

Definition of Dyslexia

Introduction

Before we can begin to discuss how to use the technology to teach and support dyslexic individuals, we need to consider the term 'dyslexia', for what is the point of discussing something if there are misunderstandings about the subject? We need to be clear what the problem is before we can attempt to solve it. For this reason, this chapter provides a firm foundation for identification and the underlying cognitive functioning that may lead to dyslexia. Only once we have established this can we clearly understand what is required.

Defining dyslexia

This book is not about understanding what dyslexia is. It is about understanding the role of technology in the field of dyslexia with regard to both learning and support. However, in order to provide a fair and valid analysis, it is necessary to consider all aspects of what is being reviewed. So let us begin with a suitable definition of what dyslexia is. Unfortunately, as many who work in this field know, that simply does not exist.

It could be argued that it is important to define dyslexia, because we need to contextualize the technology to the dyslexic individual. But it is more fundamental than that. If we do not know what dyslexia is, how can we know what kind of support to give? Furthermore, if two technology assessors have different views on what dyslexia is, they will provide different solutions to the same problem, both of which might offer some help, but neither of which is as effective as it could be. Some have argued that it is this lack of clarity and agreement on the definition that has prevented the implementation of full support that other disabilities enjoy.

To provide a baseline for discussion, let us focus on one published definition, that of the European Dyslexia Association, the full version of which is shown in the box below. However, before we dissect it, we need to decide what a definition is.

A definition is an attempt to create a simple balance whereby, on one side, there is a long description and, on the other, there is a single word or phrase. A good definition will provide a perfect balance. So the definition of a square is simple: it is a closed object that has four equal sides at 90 degrees to each other. If something has those specifications, it must be a square – if something is called a square, it must have those specifications. The two sides are balanced.

Unfortunately dyslexia is a little more difficult to define, because there can be more than one underlying cause of the measurable symptom. That is, many cognitive impairments can lead to reading and writing difficulties. And that is the key to the whole field – every dyslexic individual is different, and each individual has to be supported in a different way. If a person is labelled as 'short-sighted', then we know what to do. The label is a clear identification of the problem, and the solution is directly related and specified when measuring the problem. But if you force the person to wear glasses with the wrong prescription, then you may ruin his or her sight. Fortunately, he or she can tell you quickly if his or her eyesight is better or worse. Give a dyslexic person the wrong support, and it could be a very long time before you realize it was the wrong support.

> ### The European Dyslexia Association definition
>
> Dyslexia is a difference in acquiring reading, spelling and writing skills that is neurological in origin.
>
> The cognitive difficulties that cause these differences can also affect organizational skills, calculation abilities, etc. It may be caused by a combination of difficulties in phonological processing, working memory, rapid naming, sequencing and the automaticity of basic skills. Alongside these issues is the ongoing challenge for people with dyslexia navigating through life in a largely non-dyslexia-friendly world.
>
> Researchers acknowledge that there are many possible causes of dyslexia, including genetics. There is no relationship between a person's level of intelligence, individual effort or socio-economic position and the presence of dyslexia. Furthermore, across Europe, the diversity of languages and the multilingual demands, socio-cultural backgrounds as well as educational opportunity, have a significant influence on the life-chances for dyslexic children and adults.

Why do we need a definition?

Robinson (1950) suggested the reasons for providing a definition include not only how a word should be used, but also a set of conditions in which something occurs. So, to use the definition above, the word being defined is 'dyslexia', and the set of conditions refers to the 'difference in acquiring reading, spelling and writing skills that is neurological in origin'. If the conditions are present, it must be dyslexia, and if dyslexia is the term being used, the conditions must be present. Miles (1995) put this differently by suggesting that the definition should also provide a guide to diagnosis. This rightly suggests that if you wish to prove somebody is dyslexic, all you have to do is prove those conditions are present. This apparently simple assumption is fairly clear, but it has major consequences. What is remarkable is that so few people have realized how the whole process could be simplified if these approaches were understood.

Miles went on to suggest that a definition should also provide a watertight legal description that would automatically give entitlement to special help or provision. However, that could only happen if the definition also included cut-off criteria. Miles also suggested that a definition also provides an opportunity to show off one's pet theory and try to impose it on others. This, particularly in the field of dyslexia and financial provision of support, highlights one specific aspect of issues regarding definitions – that the final say of what is defined as dyslexia is in the hands of the funder! That is why it is so important to have an objective definition that is widely accepted.

Whose definition is accepted?

This may not be quite as clear as it seems, so let us investigate further. Let us say that an individual is assessed as dyslexic by an educational psychologist (EP), and a report is sent to the local educational authority to request funding to support the dyslexic individual, maybe including assistive technology. The authority (or 'potential funder') can either fund the request or reject it. If the authority rejects it, it can claim that it has no funds, that it does not recognize dyslexia or that the report does not prove the individual is dyslexic. We can speculate about the first two but our interest lies in the last. If the funder says that the EP's report does not prove that the individual is dyslexic, but the EP thinks it does, then clearly there is a difference between the two as to how dyslexia is proved. And if the proof is about conforming to a definition, then the two parties will disagree on the definition of dyslexia.

This is a common occurrence and has led to attempts to standardize the assessment procedure, since any arbitrary judge would tend to agree with the consensus. However, these guidelines have not always been widely adopted, and have not always conformed to the highest standards. For example, if both logic and research clearly demonstrate that an IQ test is not required to prove dyslexia is present, why do some guidelines (e.g., the UK DfES HE Working Party), while not stating outright that IQ tests are mandatory, still list them on a checklist of recommended tests? (NB These tests are used for students who have already proved that they are intelligent enough to get to university.) Could the answer be a vested interest by the advisers, and those who accept these reports? It may be argued that since IQ testing requires specialist training, if the IQ test were dropped, the testing procedure could be carried out by more (less qualified) people, at a lower cost, and could lead to more diagnoses.

Sadly, the problem is further complicated by the distinction between symptom and cause. It may be argued that it is easy to demonstrate reading and writing difficulties, but this may be an effect of the environment (e.g., a poor teacher or unsupportive parents). It is more difficult to prove a problem of 'acquisition' and for this most EPs and funders will rely on educational history. To help them, and inform what needs to happen next, many EPs use a battery of tests that aim to understand the underlying cognitive functioning. But as Siegel (1989) points out, IQ tests are more a measure of learning history than of potential. And if the disability has impaired learning, then the test cannot be a fair reflection of that potential.

This is true not only of IQ tests, but also of tests of skills such as phonological skills (rhyming and alliteration) and non-word spelling. It is not quite so true of non-learned cognitive abilities, such as memory, where the level is (relatively) fixed, and what we learn are the strategies to improve the amount of information retained. (Those who hold world records for remembering random digits have been found to have the same ordinary memory skills as anybody else. It is just that they have found a trick to remembering the numbers, such as mentally walking along a path, with objects representing the order of the numbers.)

As a consequence, a funder can say that the person is 'not dyslexic enough', or does not have a reading difficulty. (An individual can have a reading ability that makes him or her appear to be as good as the next person, but he or she may have struggled to reach that level, and still have difficulties in spelling, forming coherent arguments and getting his or her thoughts down on paper.) Or the funder may say that the EP has not proved the reading and writing difficulties have been caused by dyslexia. As we shall see, this has led many to consider the implications of assessment to a label, and prefer assessment with respect to an individual's needs.

Assessment to a label or assessment of needs?

The question of assessing to a label or assessment of needs has been briefly touched upon. However, the decision is usually neither logic based nor morally/socially based but is one of pragmatics. Students at university will not even get an assessment of needs if they do not have a piece of paper (accepted by the funder) that says they are dyslexic.

In schools, the situation varies. In some places, there is a desire to provide a label of dyslexia so that all parties know how to treat the child. In other schools, labelling will be avoided. But, cynically, this could be for two possible reasons: (a) by understanding needs, they can target specific support areas and avoid labels that can create self-fulfilling prophecies; or (b) by avoiding the label, they also avoid making financial commitments.

Ultimately, the label does not indicate what the problem is, except that there is a reading and writing problem, which was known before the label was supplied. What is needed is an assessment of needs, whether it is in one-to-one phonics teaching, or in deciding which type of concept mapping software is best. So, if a label is provided, a report of needs is still required. The label is only the first step in the diagnosis, the needs then require to be identified.

So why don't we remove the label? The answer is that it provides a common understanding developed over the years through various media campaigns, programmes, research and discussions. In the workplace, it is easier to say to your colleagues that you are 'dyslexic' than to specify the areas where you have difficulty. It is easier for a parent to understand when they are told their child is dyslexic than to comprehend the implications of 'poor phonological analysis skills and difficulties with working memory, although the visuo-spatial sketchpad is fine'. It also is easier to look up on the internet. (There are almost 8 million entries in Google for 'dyslexia', 239,000 for 'reading difficulties' and only 32,800 for 'phonological analysis'.)

But now we need to return to the definition, and analyse it, including, where appropriate, making reference to the area of computers and computing, in the widest sense.

Analysis of the EDA definition

> Dyslexia is a difference in acquiring reading, spelling and writing skills that is neurological in origin.
>
> (Smythe 2004)

Most of this seems fairly uncontroversial, since it clearly states that reading, writing and spelling are the areas of interest. These are referred to as the symptoms. For greater clarity, some definitions talk about accuracy and fluency (e.g., the British Psychological Society (BPS) 1999, and the International Dyslexia Association (IDA) 2002) with respect to these literacy skills. However, while the BPS and IDA use the term 'difficulty', the EDA use the term 'difference'. This demonstrates progressive thinking and acknowledges that we are talking about a series of neurological differences that aggregate to a difficulty in learning to read and write. Unfortunately, while this may be acceptable across Europe (for the EDA membership), in some cases it will cause a problem which the authors of the definition clearly had not appreciated.

The problem is that the word 'difference' means just that. It does not indicate disabled. And, if we accept that everybody is different, you either have to support everybody or support nobody. Since, despite lip service to the social model, funders will not support everybody, it means that if this definition were strictly enforced, nobody would be supported.

This use of the term 'difference' comes from pressure from dyslexic individuals who do not wish to be labelled as disabled, but seen as different. Some dyslexic individuals say that it is society that is disabled, not them. However, the support that dyslexic students receive from the government in the UK comes from the Disabled Students Allowance (DSA). Therefore, logically, if you accept that dyslexia is a difference and not a disability, then you cannot receive a grant from the Disabled Students Allowance. More than ten years ago, through pressure from groups such as the British Dyslexia Association, it was argued that dyslexia conformed to the 1995 Disability Discrimination Act's definition of a disability, which was 'a physical or mental impairment which has a substantial and long-term adverse effect on ... ability to carry out normal day-to-day activities'. To now use a definition that refers to dyslexia as a 'difference' instead of a 'disability' is to jeopardize the potential to receive financial support through a disability funding stream.

Note that this does not impact upon most member states of the EDA, since they do not have an equivalent to the DSA. In countries where there is state support, this wording of the definition may cause difficulties in future if used as a reference point.

Many definitions of dyslexia are restricted to this simple symptom-based part. This avoids any discussion of cause and other debatable aspects. Unfortunately all still suffer from one problem: the lack of operational criteria. Even if you have clearly stated (and everybody agrees) which symptoms must be present, you still need to be able to set this criteria. That is, if you are going to provide a label of who is dyslexic, then you must have agreed cut-off criteria in order to say who is not dyslexic.

The EDA definition continues:

> The cognitive difficulties that cause these differences can also affect organisational skills, calculation abilities, etc. It may be caused by a combination of difficulties in phonological processing, working memory, rapid naming, sequencing and the automaticity of basic skills. Alongside these issues is the ongoing challenge for people with dyslexia navigating through life in a largely non-dyslexia-friendly world.

This attempts to list the underlying cognitive causes, although a lack of clarity makes it difficult to analyse. For example, what are the 'basic skills'? Does this refer to reading and spelling, or underlying processes such as sound–letter correspondence? If the latter, then why mention phonological processing since it should also therefore be considered a 'basic process'? And what about auditory and visual memory, which are distinct from working memory? Furthermore, rapid naming is a compound skill which includes articulation and concentration. Thus, while the definition attempts to provide a guide to underlying causes which may inform diagnosis (Miles 1995) and gives more insight into how to provide support, it still leaves a lot to be desired. These issues are relevant to the discussion of ICT since they can impact not only upon the needs analysis but also will be reflected in the choice of which tests should be included in an e-assessment procedure.

Note that the relationship between literacy skills and these cognitive difficulties will be discussed later.

The remainder of the EDA definition is:

> Researchers acknowledge that there are many possible causes of dyslexia, including genetics. There is no relationship between a person's level of intelligence, individual effort or socio-economic position and the presence of dyslexia. Furthermore, across Europe, the diversity of languages and the multilingual demands, socio-cultural backgrounds as well as educational opportunity, have a significant influence on the life-chances for dyslexic children and adults.

This highlights the pervasive impact of the difficulties, and that, irrespective of cultural or linguistic background, difficulties can occur.

In conclusion, when adopting a definition of dyslexia, the EDA definition can be considered to be a good starting point. However, the use of the term 'difficulties' is contentious in that it might undermine the support principles. Therefore, an alternative version will be used here:

> Dyslexia is a difficulty in the acquisition of fluent and accurate reading, spelling and writing skills that are neurological in origin.
>
> (Smythe 2006)

Note the inclusion of 'fluent and accurate'. Although it may be argued that this is implicit, it has been emphasized for particular use in diverse language environments where the impact of fluency and accuracy on dyslexia identification can change.

Terminology: dyslexic versus dyslexia

Some people have suggested that dyslexia definitions are written by non-dyslexic people since clearly they fail to provide any real understanding of the problems dyslexic individuals face. However, the confusion arises over the difference between 'what dyslexia is' and 'what the difficulties of the dyslexic individual are'. Without going into too much detail, it is reasonable to suggest that dyslexia is caused by lower efficiencies in some areas of cognitive processing needed for reading and writing compared to non-dyslexic individuals. But those cognitive processes did not develop through millions of years of genetic selection. Reading uses a combination of cognitive processes that are also used in other areas. For example, memory is required not only for literacy but also for most other daily tasks. Thus, a poor memory will impact not only on reading and writing, but also on many of those other identifiers often quoted in dyslexia checklists, such as tying shoe laces, remembering multiplication tables, and taking down telephone messages. Some skills, such as orthographic analysis, are derived from more mature processes such as putting a name to an object. Some sound analyses are related to other tasks, such as syllabification and singing. And some are developed especially for the reading process – when else do we break up sounds into small parts (phonemes) than the natural pauses (syllables) except in literacy?

By ensuring the definition of dyslexia is clearly restricted to the symptoms of reading and writing, it is possible to understand the issues. It is not even necessary to state all the underlying causes in order to provide a basis of understanding of dyslexia. But if we identify the specific cognitive difficulties, then we can start to understand the range of problems and how best to solve them.

Comorbidity

This multiple use of underlying cognitive processes is also the reason why dyslexic individuals show difficulties in other classifiable areas such as dyspraxia, attention deficit disorder and dyscalculia. For example, the same processes that control the effectiveness of the memories (e.g., phonological and orthographic memories) used in reading may also affect the memory development for motor control. And, since dyspraxia is about motor skills, which in turn are related to control and motor memory, it is not surprising that many dyslexic individuals are also dyspraxic. Again, these issues are very important in the development of a needs assessment with respect to ICT, since the ability to control any device may be affected by the level of motor coordination. Put another way, a dyspraxic individual may find it difficult to use mouse-driven software. The ergonomic problems of using a touch screen or being faced with the wrong background colour on a screen will be discussed in Chapter 3.

Mathematical modelling of the dyslexia definition

In a paper published in 2005 (Siegel and Smythe 2005), I lamented the lack of precision in dyslexia. I highlighted that quantum physics produces testable hypotheses and occasionally seminal equations that stand up to scrutiny over time. These include:

Einstein's equation of general relativity: $R - \frac{1}{2}R\, g_{ab} = -8\pi G\, T_{ab'}$

Schrödinger's wave equation: $(\hat{H}\Psi = E\Psi)$

Physicists all over the world agree on the definition of the terms in these equations. There are assumptions relative to these equations that all physicists share. These equations are the product of reasoning and mathematical logic that hold up even under the closest scrutiny. They have become some of the cornerstones that are the basis of current research in physics. Unfortunately, there is no equivalent in research on reading disabilities. This does not mean it cannot happen, but it is a reflection of the diversity of approaches adopted, and the perpetuation of methodologies that appear to defy logic.

However, from a theoretical perspective, there is the potential to express the definition, or in this case the criteria for inclusion in the defined group, mathematically. Consider the following:

If $\dfrac{dL}{dt} < f(\bar{n})$, then $I = D$

For those not mathematically inclined, dL/dt means the incremental amount of learning that happens in an incremental amount of time.

Where L = literacy learning
t = time
$\bar{n}$ = mean of the abilities of the general population
$f(\bar{n})$ = is a function of the mean, e.g. ($\bar{n}$ − 2 standard deviations (SD))
I = individual
D = dyslexic

Put in plain English, if the increase in learning (dL) in a given time (dt) is less than 2SD (or whatever criteria you use) below the norm, then the person (I) can be considered to be dyslexic (D).

The problem for implementation is defining 'L', the literacy learning. Simplistically, if you used 'reading' as the measure of learning in this context, you could measure reading skills over time and compare them with the norm. Alternatively, you could use a sub-skill such as rhyming for a needs analysis/resource allocation for that specific skill. (Simply substitute dL for dR in the above, where R = rhyming skill.) Alternatively, you could combine several skill scores to produce a composite score to determine who is entitled to what, if a single value (i.e. if the individual is dyslexic or not) is needed. Using computers to monitor children's progress over time (through repeat implicit and explicit testing) will allow this to be easily measured. However, you still need to decide on what measure to use and the cut-off criteria.

Conclusion

This discussion might seem a little long and pedantic. However, it is precisely because there has been lack of clarity on the definition and associated issues that the level of support for the dyslexic individual remains at best patchy and at worst so poor compared with what legislation demands, that it is surprising that there have not been more legal cases. Apart from increased awareness, one of the key ways to improve support is though the wide availability of assessment. Technology is not the complete solution but, as we shall see in the next chapter, there is much that can be achieved if it is used appropriately.

2 Testing

Introduction

Every dyslexic individual is different, as discussed in Chapter 1. In order to understand the needs of any individual, we need to carry out testing, to identify the causes, strength, weaknesses and support necessary. Support, through an individual education plan (IEP), support plan or learning development plan, will provide the basis for the development of the dyslexic individuals, to overcome the areas of difficulty and allow them to reach their full potential. Unfortunately, the increase in the demand for effective assessments has vastly outstripped supply and, while in some areas there are now standard protocols (for example in higher education), this is not the case everywhere, for example in business. This is where technology has the potential to support the system, because it helps to overcome:

- the shortage of specialist assessors
- the lack of widely available test material
- the distance to assessment centres
- any inconsistency in service
- a mismatch between difficulties and learning needs
- high costs.

However, in order to give confidence to the user and the relevant authorities, any proposed system needs to be built on firm foundations. Hence the need to understand the testing principles.

The role of the computer in identification of literacy difficulties and their underlying causes is increasing. Wider access to computers, a better understanding of what is required in terms of testing, and the need (through legislative demands) to support all dyslexic individuals continue to promote both development and implementation of dyslexia assessment. For this reason, this subject should be of considerable interest not only to teachers but also to all education professionals, policy-makers, those working in HR departments, and those working in the area of identification and support of the dyslexic individual.

There is continuing debate about what can and cannot be achieved by ICT. But rarely do people step back, rid themselves of their (mis)perceptions, their protectionist attitudes, and their past experiences with computers. Only by thinking about the theoretical concepts, and by having a realistic understanding of what can be achieved, can we hope to offer computer-based cost-effective support to the dyslexic individual.

What should be in a test for dyslexia?

When we look at testing procedures, and in particular the validity of both paper-based and computerized tests, it is important to create some sort of framework for assessment. Using the model described in Smythe (2007), it is possible to develop a series of tests that could be used to suggest a protocol for children and adults at least at the single word reading and spelling level. Paper-based test materials are covered extensively elsewhere (e.g., Reid 2003). However, if the 'diagnosis' is to confirm the presence of dyslexia, then the underlying cognitive causes are not relevant.

In order to determine if an individual is dyslexic, all you have to do is demonstrate that the symptoms that define the term are present in the individual. Therefore, all you have to do is show that the individual has 'a difficulty in the acquisition of fluent and/or accurate reading and writing'. In other words, we need to do the following:

1. demonstrate a difficulty in reading (fluency and/or accuracy);
2. demonstrate a difficulty in writing (fluency and/or accuracy);
3. demonstrate that the problem is developmental and not due to a lack of opportunity.

> **Model of reading**
>
> According to Rack et al. (1993), a good model of reading must do the following:
>
> 1. Describe how reading develops.
> 2. Examine skills needed for reading.
> 3. Specify mental operations involved in reading.
> 4. Explain how this fits with current brain knowledge.
>
> Smythe (2004) adds that, if the model is correct, it should also:
>
> 1. Be relevant for all languages.
> 2. Form the basis of the assessment process.
> 3. Form the basis of the intervention process.

Norm- versus criterion-referenced testing

There are two types of testing: norm-referenced and criterion-referenced testing. With normed referenced testing, you want to know how an individual is doing compared with everybody else, usually because, in an educational context, you want to know if you should allocate (financial) support. That is, if John is not good at something, you may want to help him. But if everybody else is even worse than John, then it may be argued that you should support the entire class rather than just John. The process of collecting data to determine what the 'normal' student can do, and how individuals vary, is referred to as the norming process. The 'norms' may be considered to be a set of statistical tables which indicate how well an individual has performed compared with everybody else tested using the same measure. The important part is to ensure that the group tested to develop these norms is truly representative of the population.

Criterion-referenced testing means assessing what the individual can or cannot do. It helps determine what needs to be taught next, but does not compare the individual with anybody else. This type of test is extensively used in the context where the decision to support has already been taken.

Researchers in Greece found that a certain measure of intelligence suggested that all those in a rural environment were of below average intelligence. However, closer analysis showed that the data for the norming process had been collected from the children of academics, which produced a natural bias. This case study illustrates the difficulty of using norm-referenced materials. The closer the match between the background of those used for the norming population and the population being tested, the more reliable will be the conclusions. The only way to identify the 'dyslexic individuals' in the class who lack good phonics teaching would be to compare them with those who had a similar teaching input, i.e. those in the same class. That is, the norming population is those in the same class. This is similar to the issues with multilingualism, where the only way to provide a quantitative analysis of their (possible) problems is to compare them with individuals with similar linguistic and cultural backgrounds.

Norm referencing is only valid for the population that it was trialled with. So a test that was normed with university students will not be suitable for unemployed persons in vocational training without qualifications.

Norm tests can tell you how well a person is doing compared with others, and may help allocate resources. However, if you simply want to know the difficulties of an individual, you can use criterion-based tests. These tell you what the particular person can or cannot do. Frequently, such as in one-to-one tuition, the criterion-based test is adequate, since you are only interested in the progress of one individual. It also means that you do not have to look for tests that were based on the appropriate cohort.

Testing for dyslexia in multilingual dyslexic individuals is more problematic than testing in monolingual dyslexic individuals. The problem stems from linguistic background, and the lack of testing 'norms' in different language backgrounds. These 'norms' are required in order to compare what the person can do with what others with the same background would be expected to achieve. In theory, it sounds simple to construct such tests. In practice, to find enough people with the same first language, of the same age, and the same amount of prior appropriate teaching is difficult. The simple solution is to carry out a needs analysis and not attempt to provide a label. That is, if you have a child who has poor phonological analysis skills, then that is what needs to be taught, irrespective of his or her first language, prior teaching and labels. Not to support somebody who does not have phonological analysis skills when everybody else in the class does would be immoral.

However, the norming process does provide one other quality: that is, it can help demonstrate the abilities on other congnitive areas that an individual should have. We can test, first, for dyslexia, and then test for needs.

Case study 1 Poor teaching of phonics

In a South London school, all three Year 2 classes were tested with respect to reading, writing, and underlying skills such as rhyming, alliteration and memory. Using tests that had been developed using results from across the country, two of the classes were 'average', with one or two dyslexic individuals in each class. However, the third class performed so badly that they would all have been classified as dyslexic if they had been reviewed on an individual basis. Clearly, the issue in that third class was poor teaching of phonics. Intervention by a new teacher led to rapid improvement in the results of almost all those children.

Using checklists for testing

Checklists have received some bad press in the past as they are generally anecdotal rather than scientific. However, a good checklist can be highly predictive, and a useful guide to what is required. Also, although they are often an indicator for further investigation, they can be very telling in themselves. Thus, a question about note taking or remembering numbers can reflect memory skills, while the question about sounding out words can indicate a problem with phonics.

In the UK, the two most widely used paper-based dyslexia checklists are that of Vinegrad (originally published in *Educare* in 1994) and that of Smythe and Everatt, which originally appeared in the *BDA Handbook* in 2001 and more recently in the *BDA Employment and Dyslexia Handbook* (2009).

The Vinegrad test was developed with university students who replied to dichotomous questions (i.e. yes or no answers). The online version (see www.amidyslexic.co.uk/am-i-dyslexic.html – not to be confused with the online testing to be found at www.amidyslexic.com) reduces the need to do all the calculations.

The checklist of Smythe and Everatt was developed to overcome some of the difficulties with the Vinegrad test, namely:

1. Problems with outdated questions – 'When writing cheques do you frequently find yourself making mistakes?' – since few people now use cheques.
2. Difficulty of answering yes or no without over-generalizing – 'Do you find it difficult to remember the sense of what you have read?' – for most people, it will depend on the text.

3. It is difficult to be realistic with a simple Yes/No approach. Therefore, a four-point scale was used.

4. The selectivity of the group used to compile the norms limited the applicability of the test.

The checklist for the identification of dyslexia in adults, devised by Smythe and Everatt, has been found to be very useful in the identification of the dyslexic individual in different cultural and linguistic contexts. It may be found on the website for this book.

Computerization of literacy tests

Many of the reading and writing tests, and checklists mentioned here can easily be computerized. The complex part is rarely the testing – it is making a meaningful interpretation of the results that is the difficult part. Since there is considerable debate over which tests should be carried out, and how this process can be achieved, no attempt will be made to provide a definitive guide. However, a number of testing protocols will be highlighted to demonstrate how easy or difficult the process can be, and the extent to which validity is maintained. Put another way, we currently do not have accurate enough speech recognition software to test single word reading abilities, a test that is at the heart of testing of the dyslexic individual. However, there are other ways to test reading, which research suggests could be a viable alternative.

Testing the dyslexic adult

Dyslexia does not disappear when an individual leaves school. The underlying cognitive difficulties remain. However, with good support, many strategies can be put into place to help overcome those problems. But the need to understand those difficulties, and how they change with different contexts (e.g., when moving from education to the working environment) is important. The tests used in different contexts to identify the needs of dyslexic adults are often similar, with identification of underlying causes (e.g., memory) being the starting point. However, some tests will also include evaluation (usually by questionnaires) of tasks specific to their study or work environment. These are designed to help identify areas of strengths and weaknesses, and to highlight the necessary support for the individual as well as to enable those supplying the support (whether it is an educational establishment or an employer) to comply with disability legislation.

Types of testing

There is a tendency to think about e-assessment as solely focusing on literacy skills and the underlying cognitive difficulties. However, many other tests can be carried out using the computer, each of which has its own 'interest group'. That is, the person who takes the test may be given the support, but the testing may be set up by a number of players.

The testing itself can be of many different types. The key ones are:

- literacy skills
- cognitive skills
- study skills
- learner preferences
- visual stress
- keyboard skills
- executive functioning
- ICT needs
- work-dependent skills analysis.

The methods adopted will depend on a number of factors, with the following providing a guide to what is possible and how it may be carried out.

Choosing an e-assessment tool

The choice of a given e-assessment tool will depend on the needs of the assessor and/or the person being assessed. We can try to provide a framework to assist in making a choice using the questions on p. 20. However, note that there is little consistency between test developers that would allow an easy comparison to be made. Furthermore, since some of the aspects are contentious (e.g., how accurate are self-reported validation studies? How do you prove compliance?), any comparisons are, at best, of limited value. This is to be expected since these are mostly commercial products and therefore some of the information is sensitive information. However, while the Compliance with the Guidelines for the Development and Use of Computer-based Assessments (British Psychological Society 1999, see box) specifies how a test should conform to the guidelines, it does not say that the information has to be made publicly available. Therefore, it would be fair to say that if the developers claim their product conforms to the guidelines, one has to rely on the integrity of these people that what they say is true.

British Psychological Society Guidelines for the Development and Use of Computer-based Assessments

The British Psychological Society provides some basic guidelines for development of e-assessment. These can be accessed at: www.psychtesting.org.uk/downloadfile.cfm?file_uuid=64877B7B-CF1C-D577-971D-425278FA08CC&ext=pdf. The guidelines cover all aspects, from the development through to the user. The key components are:

1. The interface should be clear, legible and suit the needs of the user.
2. Clear explanations of what is being measured should be available to the user.
3. The tests should be both valid and reliable.
4. All instructions should be clear and accessible.
5. Scoring and feedback should be evidence-based.
6. All data should be stored securely and not used for reasons other than those agreed with the user.

When attempting to make an informed choice of an e-assessment tool, the main questions to ask are:

- What is the purpose of the evaluation?
- What is necessary to fulfil the evaluation?
- Will this tool do the task?
- How reliable or valid are the results?
- Does it conform to the accepted standards?
- What about accessibility and usability?
- Who will accept the evaluation?
- Will it work, given the technical constraints of the environment?
- What about technical issues?
- What happens to the data?

Although cost may influence the decision, that does not constitute a selection criterion on the effectiveness of a given test, or ability to do the task. By examining each of these questions in turn, it is possible to see their influence on the decision process, and how to use the available information to inform that decision.

The purpose of the evaluation

The purpose of an e-assessment will determine the content and the outcomes of the evaluation process. The primary reasons for testing are:

- to provide a label
- to assess skills
- to identify skill shortages
- to identify needs
- to assess knowledge.

In turn, this may be:

- for the user's own interest
- to provide proof to an authority (e.g., in a college or university) in order to obtain (financial) support, or at least a sympathetic approach
- for the user's parent or carer to provide proof to somebody else (e.g., a school)
- for an institution/funder to understand what support it needs to provide, both on an individual basis and across the institution
- for an employer to determine the type and level of support required under disability legislation.

In turn, the evaluation may also be to provide a 'dyslexia' label, or it may be to identify and allocate resources. In some cases, such as the Disabled Students Allowance, the purpose may shift from a label to needs assessment (see Chapter 1, 'Assessment to a label or assessment of needs?').

Another example related to purpose would be to measure auditory short-term memory. It is acknowledged that this should be carried out in the individual's first language (see, e.g., Smythe 2006). But what if, say, the child is from Thailand? There may be no norms for digit span in Thai. Does that mean he or she cannot be tested?

When choosing a tool, it is important to remember that assessment should be seen as a means to an end, and not the end itself. That is, you want to know how to support the individual, and not simply to know *if* you need to support them. Therefore, it is also important to consider the level of feedback expected from the assessment process. This is related to the discussion about the role of the human assessor. A standard assessment should include not only the testing, but also interpretation of the results and provision of some form of support that is specific to these problems. The best form of computer testing should also include these aspects. Thus the output should include not only an understanding of the test, and results of the individual, but also support strategies.

Tests should only be used where they can inform the process. It may not always be possible to turn the result into a teaching strategy, but some support mechanism should be possible. For example, if the auditory short-term memory is shown to be poor, one cannot expect to be able to change it. But this diagnosis helps us to understand the problems, and we can try to find strategies to overcome some of the difficulties. Some tests may be included to help demonstrate areas of strength upon which intervention can be built. This is fine, provided they are not just other tests that the individual can fail.

Item-response (adaptive) testing is of considerable interest in indentifying needs. The principle is to have a large battery of test items, but only use those that help identify the current level of skill. For example, a spelling test may have 100 items, ten for each year (e.g., ten which would indicate a reading age of 9 years old, ten which indicate reading age of 10 years old, etc.). With no prior knowledge, an item near the lowest age level could be provided, with the next being dependent upon the answer being correct, and how long it took to answer. For example, if a child was asked to spell the word 'light', the next word presented would be dependent on whether they spelled it correctly ('light'), if they spelled it phonologically correctly ('lite'), if they used the wrong rule ('lit'), or if they were wrong ('lihgt'). Even if he or she spelled it correctly, the speed of response could still determine the next question.

> ## What is a good measure?
>
> It is well established in testing circles that if you want to demonstrate that a child has a low reading speed (e.g., for provision of a reader for examinations for the dyslexic individual), you choose a test that will best demonstrate poor reading. But if you want to show he or she has a high reading speed, you use a different test. That is because there is no 'standard' test, and you can to some extent manipulate the result by choosing the right test.

Needs of the evaluation

Most of the issues are with respect to labels, norming and quality assurance. Again, there are many different contexts where these are needed, but the principles are the same. The requirement may be to fulfil a diagnosis of dyslexia, or to evaluate a series of strengths and weaknesses. Therefore, to evaluate the tool, it will be necessary to compare the claims of what the tool does with how well that matches the needs of the user. The needs of the 'user' are with respect to what is the intention of the testing. Having results for one's personal interest may be very different from those needed to access funding for support in study or in work.

Currently there are no e-assessment tools that a major funder (e.g., a local education authority) would accept as providing sufficient evidence to permit the allocation of (financial) resources. Therefore, at best, these tools can only provide an indication which can be presented to others. That said, these tools are often provided as the proof that something needs to be done, and can be the first stage towards the recommendation of a full assessment by an EP. If the results provide information that matches the needs of the user (e.g., when a classroom teacher needs to make an informed decision as to what to do, and does not need external permission to do it), then outside evaluation is not an issue. Sometimes there will be a compromise, so that more than one tool is used. This is because the test battery does not cover all the aspects required. Sometimes this means other tests, electronic or paper-based, are added to provide a fuller informed analysis.

There is no set of standards to which those who develop tests for use with dyslexic individuals have to conform. However, there are general guidelines for e-assessments from the British Psychological Society (see p. 20), but who determines if the test battery covers all the aspects required, and if it is appropriately administered and interpreted? Again, the user needs to have considerable knowledge. The issue of sensitive material mentioned above is also important. The test may well conform to the highest standards, but who should be privileged to that information if there is commercial gain to be made when you have access to it?

Reliability and validity

The problem with validity studies is that very few of them are carried out independently. In the few instances where it appears there has been an independent review, there is often a link back that suggests results are not truly independent, either because of the source of the funding of the 'independent' reviewer, or because, as an 'expert' in the field, the reviewer may already be working with them on other projects.

What should be tested?

Using recent reading models (e.g. Smythe and Capellini 2007), it would seem reasonable to suggest that if there are many cognitive functions required for the reading process, as many of those should be tested as possible in order to deduce what may be the cause. However, this could be questioned if you cannot change that functioning. Typical tests that may be found in computerized testing systems when attempting to understand the difficulties (as opposed to simply providing a label of dyslexia) include:

- reading (word and non-word)
- spelling (word and non-word)
- reading comprehension
- phonological analysis and synthesis
- phonological discrimination
- letters – sound correspondence
- orthographic skills
- auditory short-term memory
- visual and spatial memory
- working memory
- executive functioning
- visual–verbal sequencing
- speed of processing
- vocabulary (reception and expression)
- non-verbal reasoning
- verbal reasoning.

However, this should not be seen as a definitive list. Note that some developers produce computerized tests that attempt to follow the principle of human testing as closely as possible, while others use tests that correlate to these. (For example, the computer cannot be certain which word has been spoken in a single word reading test, but there are tests that correlate to this that could be used.) The question is always to what extent does the new test measure the same thing, and do the responses for the dyslexic individual fall on the same line as the non-dyslexics, i.e. could it be that the test is apparently valid for the general population, but not for the dyslexic individual?

Conversely, why do a study to demonstrate (or disprove) the validity of somebody else's test when for the same money you could develop your own? Science funding is about providing advances in the field and, while it may provide funding to prove or disprove a hypothesis or previous research, it is not interested in demonstrating the validity of a commercial product. So we end up with few tests for dyslexia having truly independent evaluations.

The issue is compounded by the results and the way the data are used is commercially sensitive information. Public access to that information may lead others to develop cheaper rival products, without the hard work and rigorous research that led to the high-cost product. Therefore, rightly, developers are reluctant to reveal all the background, not because they are worried that somebody will say their system is not perfect, but for fear of the loss of commercial advantage. With the increased interest in open source software, it is only a matter of time before widely available tests that are free, and even normed, will be available on the internet.

Note that in psychology there are usually two terms used for the term 'reliable' as used by the public. These are 'validity' and 'reliability'. In brief, for most purposes here, it is reasonable to say that validity refers to the match between what is actually measured and what is claimed to be measured, and the conclusions drawn from the results. Reliability refers to how close the initial assessment is compared with subsequent assessments.

So, strictly speaking, most of the wording above refers to validity. It is rare that a dyslexic individual will return to a test, since they are a means to an end and, once completed, there is no need for re-test. However, this will be more relevant in future as the testing process becomes more integral to the learning process. Although much of the discussion here has centred on the production of a report for implementation outside the software, there will be occasions when the results form the baseline for teaching. That is, in the same way that an EP's report will say what a child can and cannot do, it will also provide a baseline where it is possible to say at some future point if the child has achieved learning. That is, it provides evidence of value-added in the learning process. But, to prove the value added, you need to re-test and systems need to take account of practice effects. Therefore, it is important to have several sets of test items if re-testing is required, irrespective of whether it is paper- or computer-based.

From a philosophical perspective, it is important to consider what the test is being measured against. For example, a developer may try to compare the results of its computer-based testing with a paper-based version. This raises three issues: (1) is the test on computer comparable with that on paper?; (2) is the comparative test valid?; and (3) is the new test valid?

For (1), comparing paper- and computer-based tests, there is plenty of research that suggests this is the case. Although there have been a few more recent pieces of research, there has been a decrease in interest in this type of research since many consider the field already has received sufficient attention. Many of the reports date back to the mid-1990s or earlier, and therefore do not account for the improvements in technology since that time. Given that few differences were reported when testing was comparable, the improvement of the technology should not affect this. However, one of the issues raised was the need to ensure the face validity was maintained. That is, the test measured what it claimed to test and, if this was different from the paper test, then due attention should be paid to the difference. For example, if a spelling test was performed, keyboard familiarity might influence results, not just because of speed but also for reasons of stress, and the ease of correcting errors.

The traditional way to demonstrate 'validity' in a computer test is to compare results with those of a widely accepted paper-based example. However, that assumes the 'widely accepted' test is as valid as it claims. The question then becomes, which test is more valid? For example, the correlation between various (paper-based) reading tests is widely acknowledged as not very good. This is why teachers carefully choose which test to use when evaluating skill levels before testing prior to application for extra time in examination. But which test is 'correct', and what should be used in the validation study? A developer will choose a reading test that closely matches its product. What happens if other researchers use their computerized test and find poor correlation with a different reading test? Does that make the computerized version invalid? Of course not, but it does mean that caveats to validity must be added. Furthermore, consider what happens if you are attempting to make a 'matrices' test, where you have to choose the missing visual element. This type of test is often mistakenly referred to as a visual intelligence test. However, better it is called a visual reason task. Most researchers will compare their new test with a standard, widely used test such as Raven's matrices. However, how was the validity of Raven's established?

If you are the first developer of such a test, how can you achieve a reasonable correlation with another test? Unfortunately there is no correct answer to this. The only recourse developers have is to clearly state their choice of methods for the validation study. Note that the British Psychological Society Guidelines (1999) state: 'Where the CBA (Computer Based Assessment) is a computerized version of an assessment previously administered through paper-and-pencil or apparatus means, [the developers] should provide clear documentation of the equivalence between the CBA and non-CBA versions of the assessment.' However, it may be better to say 'documentation of the equivalence between the CBA and non-CBA versions of the assessment or deviations from it' with appropriate explanation. The lack of clarity over what constitutes an equivalent test which could be used to measure validity means that there will always be a question mark over the validity, up to the point when the test is accepted by use, and in turn is used (ironically) to validate other tests.

The issue of validity with respect to a dichotomous test (e.g., deciding if somebody is dyslexic or not dyslexic) is usually reflected in the ability to correctly diagnose the person. There are two possible scenarios – the person is labelled as dyslexic or not dyslexic – and these labels can be correct or incorrect. This gives four conditions: (1) correct diagnosis of dyslexia; (2) incorrect diagnosis of dyslexia; (3) correct diagnosis of not being dyslexic; and (4) incorrect diagnosis of not being dyslexic.

Outcomes are important for test evalualation. However, one should also reflect on the consequences of the false positive and false negative. In this case, the result of a false positive may provide a child with a label that the parents are not happy about. Conversely, it may also give additional support that was not needed. Few parents will turn down extra support for their child, but the label may be a concern.

Of great concern is the false negative, when the process says a child is not dyslexic and in fact they are. These dichotomous tests will often be used as a screening prior to a more in-depth test with an educational psychologist (EP). A false negative result would mean that, at least in the short term, a child would not be given the in-depth analysis that could have provided the additional tuition he or she needed.

When reviewing and comparing assessment tools, it is important to have an indication of the 'quality' of the test. The reputation of the developers is not enough. Indeed, anybody could develop a test – it is the demonstration that it has value and does what it claims that is important. The widely accepted (although not necessarily reliable) method is through independent evaluation published through the peer review process. Open access to the data (or at least a statistical analysis of them) and related documentation is the best way of making a judgement. However, researchers may not have sympathetic editors, the reviewer may not understand what they are reading, and the validation process itself is rarely independent due to financial limitations. For example, if you study 500 children using computerized assessment, and want to validate that against independent dyslexia assessments, who will fund those 500 assessments? (Typical costs in the UK may be around £300 for an individual assessment.) Therefore, the same researcher provides the validation tests, and it is difficult to separate the criteria for the 'independent' assessment from that of the computerized assessment. Put another way, if the researcher develops the test and then develops and carries out the validation study, there will be a high level of 'sensitivity', i.e. low levels of false positives and false negatives.

Accessibility and usability

It is important that the result of the testing should be a fair reflection of the process and not significantly influenced by factors that disadvantage the user. This can range from the individual struggling to read the instructions because of the print size to suffering from the glare of the screen because the background colour cannot be changed. Since the computer has the potential to offer these adaptations, there should be no reason why it is not permitted.)

The issue of response mechanisms (e.g., keyboard or mouse, drag and drop, or click) may appear to be a technical discussion, but really they are about accessibility, and ensuring that skills and not disabilities are measured.

The response mechanism can be split into hardware- and software-based. Hardware refers to the use:

- keyboard or keypad (e.g., numbers only or special reassigned keys)
- mouse – including special versions such as stationary mouse with a trackball
- touch screens – for a stylus or finger.

The quality (or accuracy) of response will depend upon familiarity and opportunity to practise the skill as well as motor control. Clearly the response mechanism to testing is related to the type of response. The types of response normally used are:

- keyboard response:
  - free writing
  - designated response (e.g., key 1 is for answer 1, or y = yes and n = no)
- mouse, stylus and finger response:
  - drag and drop
  - drop-down menu
  - location dependent
  - click one of several possible locations
  - free drawing.

Each is affected by familiarity, culture and the way it is implemented.

Acceptance of the e-assessment

If the only person who has to accept the test is the user, then the issues are fairly simple. All he or she has to do is try to interpret the information available, including recommendations, and decide if the 'quality' meets his or her minimum standards.

However, if the test has to conform to the needs of the funder, whether a local education authority, employer or some other body, the problem can be addressed in two ways: (1) review all the technical (psychometric) data, hoping that they all make sense (and are publicly available), or (2) rely on the reputation of the person leading the development. Both have their drawbacks. Understanding the details of psychometric data, as shown above, is not easy. Conversely, to rely on somebody's reputation is dangerous since it assumes that a reputation in development of paper-based tests means he or she can also develop computerized testing. This is as logical as assuming a world champion motorbike rider will also be a world champion in Formula One motor racing. Yes, there are comparable skills that will cross over. But not since Jim Surtees in the late 1960s has there been one person who has achieved both. This is because it needs specialist knowledge and skills. The same is true of test development.

Data management

Data storage and security should be considered at all times. In the UK, the Data Protection Act provides clear guidance to the use of data, and what needs to be done by both the developer and user. In principle, if the system is a stand-alone system, the onus is on the school to ensure appropriate use of the data. This will include a signature by the parent to say the testing can be carried out, and how the data will be used/stored and who has access to them. There should be clear guidance as to who can see which data. For example, parents should have access to their child's results but nobody else's. The classroom teacher should have access to results of their class but only the SENCO (and the head teacher) should be entitled to see the results of all classes.

When the information is stored offsite, the onus shifts to the provider of the service. There should be a clear indication of what is happening to the data, with an implicit agreement between user and service provider. In some cases the data are used for validation studies, publishable research or to improve the norms of the test. There is no problem with this, provided there is agreement prior to the information being used.

Case study 2 System overload

A computerized test was developed that was stored on the school server, and accessed using the school intranet. Tests on the developer's server showed perfect functioning. Tests in the morning before school had shown that a sound file loaded in less than half a second. However, when the kids started using the web for examination revision, with high levels of multimedia content, the system slowed down. Consequently, questions were taking up to 40 seconds to load. Since speed of response was a factor, the system had to be modified (i.e., all the multimedia files loaded onto local computers) to ensure all files were instantly accessible and were a true reflection of the person's ability rather than the connection speed.

Other e-assessments

Many tests are used by assessors, some of which are easier to computerize than others. While this is not the place to review them all, some are worth considering here, particularly as they are highly relevant to the dyslexic individual.

Study skills

Study skills refer to the effective way of learning. Research (Zhu and Smythe 2009) suggests that there are four key areas, namely:

1. Reading and writing
2. Listening and note-taking
3. Examinations
4. Time management.

These skills can be variously measured, such as through questionnaires and cognitive skills testing (including executive function such as planning and organization skills).

Learner preferences

Although there has been a recent backlash against the proliferation of 'learning styles' type systems, most of which do not have any validity, there is still some value in understanding the issues around learner preferences. One such use is the increased awareness of one's own learning, and thereby an understanding of the impact of a given teaching style.

Visual stress

Another area of increasing interest is visual stress, particularly that caused by the reading process. These difficulties can range from mild discomfort to severe migraines. Working with computer screens is a major cause of such discomfort. Reports suggest that 20 per cent of the population may suffer from visual stress. While we do not know the cause, there are tests that can identify combinations of colours that cause visual stress. (See chapter 6 for more details.)

Work skills

The evaluation of key skills for work placement is a relatively new field, with much of the 'output' dependent upon questionnaire-style evaluation. This will become an increasingly important area, particularly in times of recession. However, there will always be a question about their validity, as much of the work is about what seems right, rather than a scientific approach.

Outputs

One of the advantages of a computerized assessment is that the objectivity (and subjectivity) are consistent for everyone, since the computer merely records responses and produces outputs defined in terms of a set of conditions. However, the format of the output must conform to certain criteria, or which the most important is that it is accessible to the user group, in other words, dyslexia-friendly.

The main points to make an assessment dyslexia-friendly are as follows:

- *Re-accessible*: the user needs to have the results stored and have an opportunity to access them again at a later date. This removes the concerns about paperwork being lost.
- *Using sound versions*: it should be possible to listen to the report, either through supply of a sound file, or by ensuring it can be accessed through text-to-speech software.
- *Simple language*: the language needs to be understandable and not wrapped in psycho-babble.
- *Informative*: an assessment should lead to a clear set of outcomes in terms of learning/training and support. Providing a set of scores is only half the work.
- *Rapid reponse*: in fully computerized systems this is not an issue and offers a major advantage to the learning enviroment.

Assessing technology needs

There are many ways to make decisions about what technology should be used. The following is the model developed by Patrick Mulcahy (Consultant, ETAT (SE) Ltd), as part of an initiative commissioned by Paul Dilley and his team at the Central London Assessment Services (CLASS), University of Westminster. It is built on years of experience and provides a basic requirement in developing a report of needs. However, choosing specific software and hardware is down to the knowledge of the individual assessor.

Statement of Aims

The remit of this report is to identify the additional expenditure.

[Student Name] is obliged to incur in order to attend a designated HE course because of a disability or specific learning difficulty.

All recommendations made within this report must:

- be in respect of expenditure not covered elsewhere in Student Support Regulations;
- arise from attending or undertaking the course as well as from the disability/specific learning difficulty.

Recommendations must not be made for:

- disability/specific learning difficulty related expenditure which [Student Name] would incur irrespective of whether or not [he/she] was a student;
- course-related costs that any student would incur;
- expenditure relating to equipment or services that might reasonably be expected to be provided by [Student's Name] institution under other legislation such as the DDA.

A. Background information

- Disability (including any relevant medical conditions)
- Previous education/employment details
- Statement of course content in relation to study requirements.

B. Effects of disability on study

- Analysis of the impact of issues identified in the diagnostic report note with respect to the specific domains of research, composition, proofreading, note-taking, time management and organization, examinations and assessment.

C. Assessment outcomes and recommendations

- Detailed descriptions of study support requirements indicating evaluation decisions and strategies discussed.
  - C-1 Equipment Currently in Use
  - C-2 Recommended Equipment-based Support Strategies
  - C-3 Personal Support – Non-medical Helpers
- IT Training for recommended enabling strategies
- Non-subject-specific study skills tuition (one-to-one support)
  - C-4 Support Materials, Consumables and Accessories.

Heisenberg's Uncertainty Principle and testing

In quantum physics, Heisenberg's Uncertainty Principle states that you cannot accurately know both the speed (or momentum) and the position of a particle at the same time. Heisenberg suggested that the very act of observation changes the result, making precision impossible. In the testing process, one can find analogies:

1. You cannot test without giving instructions.
2. In providing instructions, you may be implicitly teaching.
3. If you are teaching during testing, you are influencing the measurement of that skill.

In real terms, the tester (human or computer) will usually provide a set of instructions and several examples for practice to ensure the instructions are understood. If the answer is wrong during the practice phase, there may be more instructions. However, this is (at least implicitly) teaching.

Therefore, it may be true to suggest that you cannot measure learning without giving instructions. But you cannot give instructions without providing learning. You can either know exactly the individual's ability on a task but not be sure they have understood the task, or you can give explicit instructions with practice items but be unsure how much teaching has been carried out to ensure the instructions are understood.

Computers will help, but while they will not remove this need to provide instructions (and, indeed, using computers may be even more difficult for some unless there is human support available since you cannot program every eventuality for misinterpretation), they do at least ensure everybody has the same information and the same chance of success.

Conclusion

Computers give us the power to individualize teaching, to identify areas of needs, and then to provide for that need. An experienced, appropriately trained teacher has the skills to deliver to pupils all that they need, given the time and the resources. However, the reality of the twenty-first-century educational system is that all teachers have to deal with large classes of diverse ability children with diverse needs, have a huge administrative burden, do not have time for the training they need, and are not provided with the resources necessary to do the job, even if they did have the time and training.

The development of computerized testing derives from a desire (led by both parents and teachers) to find out what the problems are. Computerized testing helps to overcome the shortage of local specialists, the lack of training, and the costs that would be involved. In the end, what it does is pinpoint the problem with reasonable accuracy. Everybody now knows the path to follow, but who will ensure that happens?

In theory, at least, the notion of independent dyslexia testing should disappear. Currently testing may lead to recommended support. In future, testing and support should be integral to the same process. As one example, in Brazil, computer-based research is being carried out that is looking to develop effective ways of teaching rhyming. The software tests the rhyming skills of the individual, builds a pattern of skills that identifies his or her rote-learned rhyming and the refinement of his or her rhyming algorithm to develop and then deliver the content of the rhyming learning plan. This plan uses the principles of item-response theory and Bayesian networks modified to accommodate the diversity of patterns found in written language (Smythe and Capellini 2007). The result is that testing and learning are integral. Simpler versions of this are already in place, but rarely do they suggest they can target the specific skill so clearly. Most work on simple repetition and fulfilment of the overall task at an appropriate level. The aim of the above proposal is to integrate it into a single system that also teaches all aspects of spelling, but in a way that is implicit rather than explicit. That is, the text the children see on the screen (e.g., if they are reading a story) is constructed based on their previous 'test results'.

However, this should not suggest that the integration of testing and teaching is just around the corner. Far from it. Considerable progress has been made possible thanks to the computational abilities of computers. But there is still lots to learn about the basics of how children learn. Connectionist theories have provided some insight, but have not provided much in the way of solutions. Until we have a better understanding of how kids learn, we cannot hope to deliver effective teaching. Computerized assessment can offer some support in this. It has the potential to deliver results from huge numbers of individuals so that we can map the relationship between underlying cognitive skill deficits and the outcomes in terms of literacy strengths and weaknesses.

If we do away with the need for a specific label, be it dyslexia, dyspraxia, dyscalculia, dysmemoria, dysalliterationia or whatever new theory comes into fashion, and concentrate on skill strength identification and development, there is an opportunity for progress. To continue arguing about the criteria for identification of dyslexia, which was first identified over 110 years ago, highlights the lack of progress in the field.

Furthermore, it shows how many people are really missing the point. The point is to find out what is the cause of the difficulties, and find ways to teach in a manner that overcomes those difficulties. We do not need more research on thousands of children to suggest the difference between dyslexic and non-dyslexic individuals. That will not help any dyslexic individual. All that can help them is identification of their specific needs; only then can we hope to support them. We can use computerized testing to help tease out the answers, because the computer can be objective, can collect large amounts of data, can be non-threatening and can rapidly analyse the results. However, it still relies on the skills of the researchers to be as objective as possible (as opposed to pushing their pet theories), and to ensure the quality of the recommendations.

For now, we should celebrate the advances made in the past ten years, and hope that at least in the short term the outputs of computers will be linked realistically to those areas discussed in the rest of the book, without compromising the more human side of learning!

3 Assistive Hardware

Introduction

As soon as you make a specific recommendation, the technology (and terminology) will change. As laptops become netbooks and webbooks, and phones have built-in projectors, it is important to reflect on needs and how they can be fulfilled. This chapter is about identifying components, making choices and getting the best from those choices for the dyslexic individual. The traditional way to discuss hardware that is relevant to dyslexia and the dyslexic user is to list the different devices and what they can do. However, the rapid rate of technological change means that the role of any one piece of equipment may change as its technical capability (e.g., resolution or sensitivity) improves, and the distinction between components becomes blurred. Therefore, the aim here is to provide an overview of the major components, the impact of their specification on the dyslexic user, and how this might change over the years.

Technical processes

Although later in the chapter we shall consider hardware in this traditional manner, let us start by considering the processes of what we are attempting to do.

Technology, at least within the realm of dyslexia support, can perform five distinct roles:

1. Capture information
2. Analyse information
3. Store information
4. Synthesize information
5. Output results

All this is using the full potential of multisensory multimedia presentation. While software processes the information, hardware captures and provides a means to output the results in the most effective manner. In presenting the hardware, we shall review their roles, characteristics and how they are changing, in order for us to make informed choices at every stage.

What is a computer?

A computer may be considered to be a device that accepts and manipulates data according to a set of instructions, and provides an appropriate output. Computers are now so ubiquitous that we do not really need to think about what they are, in most cases. With technology improving the computer's capability to perform more complex calculations in shorter times, at lower costs, our definition of what a computer is becomes blurred. The humble microwave oven now contains more processing power than the Apollo rockets that went to the moon in 1969. The average smart phone has more multimedia handling capability that most desk-based computers had five years ago. The introduction of products with marketing jargon such as netbooks and webbooks, suggesting ultra-portability with restricted use, proved to be a short-term distinction as the principles of portability were more widely adopted and built-in processing power was increased. With software running from memory cards, and mobile phones having built-in projectors, it is easy to see differences between technologies becoming blurred.

Yet most of the tasks computers need to deal with on a daily basis could still be performed on the same computers that were available more than ten years ago. (The exceptions are those that require high-end video graphics.) For example, word processing is really a very simple task that could be carried out with very slow systems and some of the better-known software for assessment and learning was originally developed ten years ago to operate with far less sophisticated systems than we have today.

The significant changes that have occurred are in graphics handling, particularly in terms of the speed to calculations carried out to create new scenes in computer games in real time. Data handling for audio has also played its part, although for most applications the slower speeds still work well. It is only with the more sophisticated software such as speech-to-text that processor speed becomes important. However, unless you need these specific tools, the only thing that drives the faster machines is the hype that creates the apparent need for more sophisticated machines, and the consequential lack of support for the older machines.

The proof of this superfluous speed is that so much software is now being accessed through the internet, where connection speeds are clearly a lot less than on the stand-alone computer. The real processing is being carried out on remote servers and, in all probability, the processing power we need locally is no more than what was available five years ago. What has changed is the supporting software programming techniques. The components that will remain local need only be the sending/uploading of data (keystrokes, files, voice, mouse movements and images) and rendering so the data can be seen (on a screen or projected) and heard. The massive chip speeds, processing power and storage capacity currently available will be largely redundant in terms of a world that operates online. In future, the master of processing will be connection speed. The secret will be to avoid being the slave to the connection.

Computer components

If we look at the computer in detail, we can appreciate it like a good hi-fi system. In the past you had a turntable, a cassette player, a radio and an amplifier. If you wanted the best, you could mix and match from different manufacturers. When CDs became popular, you could add that component and remove the redundant parts. And you could plug in the mp3 player to a socket hidden away at the back. But if you were happy with an integrated system, which was of a reasonable quality but had everything, you could accept the compromise. Computers are like this. The problem is that most people tend to treat them as the integrated compromise. To understand this better, let us consider the standard computer, and how we can modify the 'computing environment' to become more user-friendly.

There are four main components to a 'computer':

1. the processor (the worker)
2. the monitor (output, or input if it is a touch screen)
3. the keyboard and mouse (input)
4. the memory (storage).

The processor

Moore's law suggests that computer chip capability doubles in function every two years. Even apparent limits due to the principles of physics have been overcome by changing the technology, thereby retaining this law. The latest super-computers that hold the world record for speed use the technology developed for the hand-held games industry. When we choose a computer, details of the processor are usually seen as a function of marketing. However, there are some fundamental differences in the way that processors work, and this should be considered when making choices. The basic difference concerns parallel processing. Put simply, either you can do things in sequence (serial processing) or you can try to do several things at once (parallel processing). The recent advances in speed are about the development of more advanced parallel processing algorithms and their related technology, plus smaller units meaning less distance for the signal to travel, and therefore faster reaction. I have no intention of suggesting what would be best, since the technology advances so rapidly that whatever is suggested now would be obsolete within a year. However, high-end graphics, computer gaming and especially speech-to-text require high levels of number crunching that can only be achieved through the most advanced parallel processors.

The monitor

Traditionally, the dyslexic individual prefers a larger text size on the screen. Obviously, this means that less information can be seen at any one time. In many cases this could be an advantage as it allows one to concentrate on the information in the viewable area and not be distracted. However, there may be occasions when it is better to have a large viewable area. One example would be to see all parts of a concept map at the same time, and at a readable size. At times like this, the large screen is preferable. High screen resolutions improve clarity, but it is the combination of screen size, screen resolution and distance from the screen that should be considered.

Small screen netbooks

The introduction of small screen sub-notebooks/netbooks reiterates the need to pay careful attention to the monitor. Although these screens are at a resolution that was the norm ten years ago (typically 600 pixels high, although increased from 800 to typically 1024 pixels wide), the pixels are a lot finer, and you need to crouch over the computer to read it easily. However, it is easy to attach a large external monitor to a small computer, and even an external keyboard, making the small computer less restricting. Thus the issue is not about 'dual' monitors, but temporary monitor substitution.

The problem with these small computers is that most common software (e.g., the browser and Office programs) take up a lot of space at the top of the screen with menus, thereby reducing the working area. This can be very inconvenient with the smaller laptops.

Author's Choice: Models change so rapidly that there is no point telling you what I recommend. But I can tell you that I use a Windows XP machine, with a 10-inch screen, over 6 hours of battery life and three USB points, but no internal CD/DVD drive. It is 600 x 1024 pixels. It weighs just 1.1 kg and is perfect for carry-on luggage for all the travelling I do. It is perfect for short-term use.

Touch screens

There is now a good range of computers with touch screens, at affordable prices. This could change the way we interact with computers in the near future. The obvious advantage is that you no longer have to split concentration between looking at what is happening on the screen and checking your keyboard.

However, some dyslexic users prefer to have the tactile feedback from the computer, as the key depresses and they can feel when more than one key is being touched. Furthermore, the skill of correct finger placement on a perfectly flat screen may tax some dyslexic individuals. This is only slightly relieved by using a stylus.

Furthermore, stylus-led typing, such as used on many PDAs and smart phones, lacks the implicit learning of typing through fingers. Any experienced typist will tell you that they do not have to think about spelling too much as the fingers seem to know which keys to push. The reason is that with practice the brain builds a pattern that turns the sound or written lexical entry into a finger sequence. That sequence is about moving ten fingers in a clear pattern. A dyslexic individual can learn to type, although the speed of learning may be slower, and the quality of those brain patterns, or engrams may be lower. The stylus, however, is a single point of contact, and the pattern development does not happen, irrespective whether the individual is dyslexic. Consequently the need to search the keyboard remains. Typing and the problems it causes dyslexic individuals are discussed in Chapter 4 on assistive software.

There is little doubt that in the next few years many resources will be designed for the touch screen. This will make testing more realistic, and will cause many developers to reconsider the response method of their tests and games. There is a conceptual difference between watching your finger touch the screen at the appropriate place, and moving the (unseen) mouse while you watch the cursor move on the screen. Touching will be easier and faster, requiring a lot less processing that will interfere with the intended area to be measured. This use of touch screens may lead to a need to re-norm tests as responses may be very different.

Many dyslexic users will also have dyspraxic tendencies, and therefore may not have as much control over their actions when using a touch screen. This may be a function of visual perception or motor control. Irrespective of the cause, this may lead to screens being broken due to the over-enthusiastic use of a stylus, or because it was knocked over because the individual did not have enough control over the pressure they needed to use.

The new no-touch touch screen

An extension of the traditional touch screen is the '3D' touch screens which detect proximity to a point. This may be of use to many, with the cursor/response changing depending on how near the finger is to the screen. However, for the dyslexia individual with dyspraxic tendencies, this will almost certainly be a nightmare since the degree of precision needed may be considerably greater than they can manage.

Dual screens and virtual desktops

Films such as 'Minority Report' gave credibility to the technical possibilities of using multiple screens, even if their implementation was a little stretched. But it does highlight the issue that while many people push for higher speeds and better quality monitors, nobody has addressed how you can create the technological equivalence of spreading the books out on the floor. One 'solution' is to use two screens instead of the usual one. That is, you can increase the size of the visual working area by connecting a second screen (and appropriate software if necessary) to the standard screen. This could allow you, for example, to write a report on one screen while viewing the spreadsheet with the necessary data on the other screen. The traditional way is to have several windows open at once and click through them. The problem with this is that the dyslexic individual will have problems remembering where information is as they swap between active windows. The dual screen facility is very useful for desktop computers, but is particularly good when the main computer is a small laptop. The second (non-portable) screen can become the principal screen in the home, thus relieving potential eye strain and back strain.

The keyboard, mouse and other input devices

Most people never change the keyboard that comes with the computer, whether it is a desktop version or a laptop. Why? The answer is a combination of laziness, a failure to appreciate the alternatives, and a lack of understanding of the impact it could make. But it is also a case of what you get used to. Many people use just the standard alphanumerics, and fail to take advantage of the full potential of Function keys, Print Screen, the Windows key, etc.

Function keys in Word

Function keys provide a short-cut in some programs for a special routine. Rather than seek a common activity through the drop-down menus, all you need to do push a single button. In Word, the keys are assigned as follows:

F1	Get Help or visit Microsoft Office online.
F2	Move text or graphics.
F3	Insert an AutoText entry (after Microsoft Word displays the entry).
F4	Repeat the last action.
F5	Choose the Go To command (Edit menu).
F6	Go to the next pane or frame.
F7	Choose the Spelling command (Tools menu).
F8	Extend a selection.
F9	Update selected fields.
F10	Activate the menu bar.
F11	Go to the next field.
F12	Choose the Save As command (File menu).

However, few people use these. One reason is that their assignment changes for each program, and dyslexic users do not like to remember what happens in which program. That said, there is no reason why some form of 'crib sheet' could not be attached to the top of the keyboard. (Key assignments can also be modified in Word through Tools/Customize/Options/Keyboard.)

Each keyboard has its own advantages (and disadvantages). For example, the roll-up type tends to have a very different feel from conventional keyboards, and may not suit many users. Furthermore, the space it takes up is marginally smaller than a standard keyboard, making it only a novelty. However, it can be a considerable bonus with children who spill drinks or have temper tantrums around keyboards.

Using Prt Scr as data rescue

Print Screen (usually labelled Prt Scr) can be a useful tool when a program freezes and there is a danger of losing your work. If you hit Prt Scr, it will capture an image of the desktop which may be saved in another program. However, be warned that you cannot simply drop the image into any program since many need to be open before you hit Prt Scr, and opening the new program may prevent you taking a Print Screen of the lost data. Therefore, test the system before you need it. One free program that does all this is RIOT (Radical Image Optimization Tool; http://luci.criosweb.ro/riot/).

The Print Screen is a very useful function that is little understood. A simple illustration will help: a tutor is attempting to demonstrate how to do something (e.g., how to access some information through the internet using a specialist search engine). The steps are complicated but consistent. The dyslexic user would not be able to remember them, nor write down clear instructions fast enough. So each time there is new information, the Prt Scr key is pressed. This captures everything that is on the screen at that time. Each time the Prt Scr is used, they then paste (Ctrl V) into PowerPoint, and what was seen is saved. (If the area of interest does not occupy the full screen, then Alt Prt Scr can be used.) This allows you to return later to check the instructions. NB You could also do this as a 'video' screen capture, but files can be big, with lots of 'nothing'.

The 'virtual' keyboard is also more novelty than useful, but is worthy of mention. Basically, a laser projection is made onto a surface from a small device about the size of a mobile phone. The keyboard layout appears on the surface, and you can type using this technique. But the lack of tactile feedback makes it very difficult for the dyslexic (and dyspraxic) individual to learn how to use it. A high degree of manual control and confidence is required to use this effectively. With projectors being built into mobile phones, we may well see greater use of this type of control, at least as a 'virtual mouse' for navigation, if not the full keyboard. But it is more likely that alternative folding keyboards will dominate as a 'lifesaver'.

 Author's Choice: I like the feel of the keyboard on my laptop but prefer the functionality of a stand-alone. However, I have yet to find a stand-alone keyboard as user-friendly (quiet, small, good for travel) as the laptop version.

Fold-up keyboards are an excellent way to use the full note-taking and writing potential of the smart phone and will no doubt become more widely used as people start to use projector phones more widely. The on-phone keypads (3 x 3 or full keyboard) can be used with speed but cannot be as speedy as using two hands on a keyboard. The fold-up keyboard, which can be carried in a jacket pocket or handbag, offers portability and a useful technological addition to the individuals who feel left out as they cannot use their skills fluently with the mobile keypads due to motor difficulties.

Dvorak keyboards (see box) offer an alternative layout that may suit some people. However, if the traditional keyboard has already been learned, the dyslexic individual may have trouble adapting to the new layout. The advantage of the Dvorak keyboard is that the layout takes account of letter frequency, whereas the standard layout owes much to the need to have keys set in a way so that the mechanisms of the old mechanical typewriters did not entangle themselves in certain combinations when used by fast typists.

Keyboard layout

There are a number of different layouts, but generally only two can come with the Windows and Mac operating systems. These are the QWERTY and Dvorak systems. The original layout was designed to minimize the key jams that used to occur with the original mechanical devices.

In the 1930s, August Dvorak developed an alternative layout based on letter frequency and combinations as well as physiological considerations. However, some studies suggest that it is difficult to recuperate costs for retraining. But the apparent reduced likelihood of wrist strain has led a number of individuals to learn to use a Dvorak keyboard rather than the traditional QWERTY keyboard.

In the 1970s, Lilian Malt re-examined the strain issues, and in collaboration with Stephen Hobday developed the Maltron keyboard (www.maltron.com). Their analysis of the logic behind the keyboard makes for very interesting reading. The keyboard rest keys (i.e. those keys where the fingers naturally rest) on the QWERTY – ASDF : HJKL – allow just 27 words to be typed.

However, with the Maltron layout rest keys – ANISF : DTHOR – over 7500 words can be typed. For the 20 most common words (*the, of, and, a, to, in, is, you, that, it, he, was, for, on, are, as, with, his, they, I*) which account for 25–30 per cent of all words used in English, only 'a' can be typed with the rest keys using a QWERTY layout, while all but four (*you, was, with, they*) can be typed using rest keys with the Maltron layout.

In some circumstances it may be desirable to have a single key specially assigned. The Microsoft Keyboard Layout Creator is a free tool that allows the layout to be adjusted. (A keyboard layout manager is available at www.klm32.com/index.html. However, compatibility with Vista is uncertain.

Of mice and touch pads

Movement across the screen face (location response systems) can involve the use of the mouse, touchpad and, as previously mentioned, the touch screen. You can also use the keys for navigation, particularly with web pages. For the dyslexic individual, the choice usually comes down to practice and preference rather than technical specification. With some mouses (should it be mouse – like the plural of sheep is sheep – mouses or mice? Who should be the authority?), the response can be changed by the user. Thus, a large movement of the mouse can have less effect on screen. This is also true of the touch pads. The two main types of mouse are the 'traditional' and the 'upside-down' mouse, there the device is fixed and the ball is moved to create screen movement. This is usually referred to as a trackball (or rollerball) mouse. Some dyslexic (and dyspraxic) individuals prefer the latter, although there is no advantage to either.

Touch pads are the most common form of movement control on laptops, although some producers use a micro-joystick embedded in the keyboard. These joystick versions tend to be more difficult for the dyslexic user due to their greater need for 'feel', and a stop–go action that can be frustrating. Like all skills, given time, this technique can be mastered. But if you have a choice, joysticks should be avoided. The addition of a traditional mouse through one of the USB ports offers a simple solution.

Experience shows that many dyslexic individuals will use the mouse for such common tasks as 'Save', seeming to prefer the slower and more difficult task of navigating to the appropriate drop-down menu to the faster alternative of using a short cut (e.g., Ctrl S for 'Save' in most programs). The reason is one of memory and familiarity. However, teaching common short cuts can relieve much frustration, especially when dyspraxia (motor control of the mouse) is an issue.

Memory/storage

Traditionally, you stored your data on the computer you were working on. However, that is changing in several ways. Cheap flash (USB) memory sticks (cost per gig is about the same now as the cost per meg five years ago!) mean that it is easy to move information from one machine to another, as well as have a back-up system. On the plus side it makes back-up easy, and you are not restricted to one computer. On the downside, it is easy to lose memory sticks. The answer would be to have a simple piece of software that works in the background which automatically saves to the computer hard drive and to the memory stick. Then keep it safe, for example by attaching it to a set of keys or the mobile phone.

Second, the push has been towards online working, with the potential for online document production and storage, or at least back-up being made to an online system, finally being realized. However, while it may be good to work online, it is important to be able to download the document and work on it offline when there is no connection. (Imagine the businessman on a 6-hour plane journey who has no internet connection. An online system is of little use unless an offline version is also available.) This dual function (and storage) is beginning to be understood, but is not yet widely implemented.

How often do you back-up?

Most importantly, you have to remember to back-up. In a straw poll I found, 'Once in a blue moon' was the most common answer (around 30 per cent), alongside 'Never' (also 30 per cent). Only 10 per cent did it daily (probably corporately).

Backing up

Five good reasons to have a second set of files stored away from the main computer:

1. The computer could be stolen.
2. The computer might crash and become inaccessible for a few days.
3. The hard drive may die for inexplicable (technical) reasons and become inaccessible forever.
4. The computer may suffer a sad end, such as fire, water, earthquake or be knocked off a desk.
5. You go somewhere that does not have access to the computer.

When it comes to 'back-ups', we can ask why we need them. We can classify them into two main types:

1. We know where the data are/were, but unexpectedly no longer have access to it (see scenarios 1–4).
2. We go somewhere knowing we will not have access to the computer (see scenario 5, which could be because we do not want to drag a computer around, such as on a trip abroad).

Author's Choice: For major system back-ups, I use a large hard drive (320 gig) external hard drive, and store in a place separate from the computer.

For day-to-day back-ups I use a USB memory stick. Until recently these have not been an option for full back-ups. But at 32 gig, this goes a long way towards a reasonable long-term back-up. It stays with my keys and is unlikely to be lost at the same time as my computer.

More recently I have been using online storage with automated back-up. This has the added option of letting me have access to data any time I have internet access.

Choosing a laptop

The criteria used for choosing a laptop are very similar to those used for choosing individual components. Some companies online even allow you to choose your specifications. For the dyslexic user, 'comfort' and 'familiarity' may be as important as specification. Furthermore, it is important to try to avoid lowering the specifications since slower speeds (especially if speech-to-text is used) will just add to the frustration. Size is usually the key, with decisions being based on trade-offs between screen size and portability.

Author's Choice: My 'laptop' is a 15 inch, which is the one I have at home but can also move around. At home, I prefer to plug into an external 22-inch (1600 x 1200) screen. It means I can see at least two full-size A4 documents at the same time.

The main (and obvious) advantage of the laptop is its portability. However, it comes at a price, which is the problem of power. A few years ago, the AlphaSmart provided an alternative where battery power would last for days, although it was restricted to about five lines of text. These were adopted extensively in the dyslexia world because they were also low cost. Unfortunately, many of these new small computers suffer from a short battery life often as low as 90 minutes as standard, because not only is the machine small but so is the battery. Although second batteries can be carried, this negates the low cost and convenience.

However, as power requirements drop and battery technology improves, we are beginning to see the emergence of long-life batteries claiming 8 hours or more. This is crucial in environments such as universities where lecture theatres seldom have adequate power supplies.

Power supplies and batteries

The desktop computer is fixed and we do not need to consider the power supply. But for other devices, especially laptop computers, it is important to remember the limited power of batteries. Although '24-hour' batteries are promised soon, they are not here yet. Sadly few places are built with the dyslexic individuals and their power needs in mind. In schools and colleges, the number of sockets is rarely enough for the number of users, and are usually limited to the walls around the outside. Therefore, the optimum place for a dyslexic student to sit, at the front or in the middle, has to be considered with respect to available power sockets.

Disability legislation ensures that universities must make adequate provision for the dyslexic individual, and many do. Interestingly, few institutions appear to have realized the relationship between laptops, the need for power and the Disability Discrimination Act. Clearly there is a duty for the institution to provide enough power sockets to support all those with laptops. However, this is rarely the case. As a consequence, often the dyslexic individuals are not able to run their computer all day.

Increasing battery life – in the short term

1. *Dim your screen* – This is an obvious way to save power, since the backlight used to light the screen accounts for 2–3 watts of power.

2. *Avoid multitasking* – Minimize the number of programs running at the same time, including those running in the background. You can see how busy your CPU is by going to the Task Manager. Decreasing the activity will increase the battery life.

3. *Minimize the number of 'devices' operating* – USB devices such as the mouse can be a power drain. Switching off WiFi saves another few watts. Run software from the hard drive, not from the CD/DVD drive.

4. *Adjust the power settings* – Use the one that maximizes battery life. This will decrease performance slightly, but not enough to show with standard programs such as word processing.

5. *Lower screen resolution* – This option decreases the call on the graphics computing. Although generally not recommended since the low resolution may be uncomfortable and counter-productive, it is nonetheless an option that could be considered.

6. *Use 'Hibernate' instead of 'Standby'* – Hibernate saves far more power than going into standby mode. Although placing a laptop in standby mode saves some power and you can instantly resume where you left off, it doesn't save anywhere near as much power as the hibernate function does.

Increasing battery life – in the long term

1. *Defrag regularly* – It is surprising how few people appreciate the importance of regular defragging. Defrag (or defragmentation) is needed because of the way the computer allocates space to files and later reallocates that space. If the chosen space is not big enough, the file is broken into several chunks. Defrag is the process of putting files back together. The impact of failing to do defrag regularly is that the computer has to work harder to find the parts of the file and put them back together, which uses more battery power.

2. *Maintain the battery and computer* – Keep battery contacts clean using alcohol, and make sure you use the battery every few weeks. Keep the device cool by ensuring fan vents are clear. Make sure the laptop rests on a hard surface and not a soft one that can close the vents.

3. *Add more RAM* – Using virtual memory takes more power than using actual RAM. However, check your machine's current capabilities compared with the software needs before rushing off to add more kit.

Most people will want the battery to last as long as possible, both in terms of years of service, and the time between charges. However, for the dyslexic individual the loss of power can present a greater challenge than to the non-dyslexic user who has the possibility of falling back on regular note-taking possibilities. In the same way that the computer can be an enabling technology, so too its loss can be disabling.

> ### Laptops, hard drives and software installation
>
> One problem of the small laptops is a lack of a CD/DVD drive for loading software. You could download it from the internet, though not ideal if you have big programs such as speech-to-text. Now some suppliers of technology for dyslexic individuals pre-load all the key software with 30 days demos.

Choosing between operating systems

Although technically it may be argued that the choice of platform is a software issue, in reality it is a hardware decision, since the platform is installed in the machine that you buy. It is not a decision you make later. The main choices are (with few exceptions) Windows, Apple Mac or Linux. However, Google Android and Chrome OS are set to take a significant market share in the near future, blurring the distinction between computers and mobile phones along the way.

Although discussed earlier, it is worth reiterating that the functionality of these is similar. However, most would agree that the Apple Mac is more intuitive and user-friendly, as well as being a computer of choice for those in or looking to enter the visual arts. This is due to the superior parallel processing of the graphics. However, the choice of a Mac may limit the software available, such as educational games for children or specialist statistical software such as SPSS. However, you can use a software-based solution to run a Windows environment on an Apple computer.

Until recently, Linux was the platform for geeks, with few people being interested in it, except large corporations running custom-made software. However, part of the reason why some of the sub-notebooks are so cheap is that there are no costs for the operating system. Most of the needs of the average user can be satisfied by using open source software, such as OpenOffice (a free version of Microsoft Office), along with Firefox and a whole host of online resources. However there are important restrictions with text-to-speech and speech-to-text. Unfortunately it is this very software that dyslexic individual uses most. As computing moves more and more towards 'The Cloud' (the term that refers to processing and storage being online), so the needs of the computer decrease as all the differences between operating systems are absorbed by the browsers.

Other devices

The technology to support dyslexic individuals is found in a range of different other devices, such as sound recording devices, mobile phones, scanners or note-taking pens.

Sound recording devices

There are many ways in which the recorder can be used by the dyslexic individual, but the main ones include:

- self-recording for reason of memory (e.g., remember to buy a present)
- self-recording of notes for transcribing later
- self-recording for speech-to-text
- recording of others in lectures, etc.
- to send messages between schools and parents
- to remember shopping lists.

Specific uses may include:

- to record homework
- to remember instructions at home, school or work
- to say ideas aloud before you forget them
- to record lessons or key parts of lessons
- communicating between home and school.

The recording can be carried out in three principal ways:

1. Using the computer (laptop or desktop).
2. Using a mobile phone.
3. Using hand-held devices.

All three have their merits, although the principles are similar. For computers, the primary concern will be the microphone and the recording software. (Free/open source software such as Audacity will cover most uses.) With mobile phones, the strengths and weaknesses will depend upon the specific make and model. They can be good for quick notes and when low quality is not a concern.

Probably the best type is the independent digital recorder built specially for the task. Ten years ago the standard device was either a micro-cassette type of recorder, or the cheaper device that used standard cassettes which needed some form of software to transform it into a usable format. Today the standard is a solid state device, with high quality recording as mp3 files that can be directly uploaded to the computer.

The usefulness of the recording is often dependent on the quality of the microphone and not the internal workings of the recorder. The built-in microphone is good for hand-held self-recording, but for recording lectures or for using with speech-to-text, a high quality directional microphone will provide much better results. Note that there are usually several settings for recording quality, which will impact upon the recording time. Twice the quality will give half the recording time.

Battery power and recorders

One of the main issues for the recorder is one of power. You can become so over-reliant on the recorder, and forget to ensure the batteries are fully charged. And batteries always fail at the wrong time. You should have a system to check them regularly in place to minimize frustration. Of course, if the device is used at the front of a lecture theatre or in a business meeting, then there is little chance of the little recording light being seen or rectifying the situation.

When it comes to microphones, try to ensure you have the one best suited to the task. The ones that come on laptops or built into digital recording devices rarely have the capability to record at the level demanded by the dyslexic individual. The principal uses will be speech-to-text and recording homework, lectures, etc. The more you pay for a microphone, the better it will be. But you have to be aware of, for example, directionality of the microphone and the impact of the loss of battery on powered microphones.

Note that when you listen to the playback on the device, the quality is often a lot better with headphones than using the device loudspeaker. If you are able to try a device in the shop (as opposed to buying online), take a pair of quality headphones and an external microphone just to see their impact, and check the real quality of the device.

> ### Ten tips for making the most of recording devices
> 1. Always use a high quality directional microphone.
> 2. Maximize the difference between the target sound and background noise.
> 3. If using a computer to record, keep separate from the main power supply.
> 4. If using a computer to record, put the hard drive to sleep mode.
> 5. When using a hand-held device, try to avoid touching it while recording.
> 6. Make sure the batteries will last long enough to do the job.
> 7. If using a battery-operated microphone, ensure the battery will last.
> 8. Make sure there is sufficient storage capacity for the task.
> 9. Download and back-up all recordings as soon as possible.
> 10. Check sound levels before starting.

Personal Digital Assistant (PDA)

The days of a PDA (or Personal Digital Assistant) as a stand-alone device are numbered. But as Jack Schofield wrote in the *Guardian* newspaper 'The PDA is dead. Long live the PDA functions' (Schofield 2007). The introduction of the PDA in the 1990s offered a badly needed personal device that could handle the needs of the dyslexic individual, particularly in a form of a single device that offered a calendar, diary, alarm and general memo pad. Despite some models having serious problems (such as losing all information when the battery died!), they were seen as a useful tool for dyslexic individuals. Their decline, which began around 2004, can be directly attributed to the increased availability and functionality of the smart phones as they began to offer some features of the stand-alone PDA, as well as improved media recording playing and email possibilities. And who wants to carry two devices when one will do? Nowadays the PDA is not seen as a device that is worth considering as an additional item for the dyslexic individual, except when they have been used for a long time and there is a comfort in familiarity.

Hand-held spellcheckers and thesauruses

While most people use the spellcheckers built into word processors such as Word, there are occasions when a hand-held spellchecker is useful, such as when writing by hand, or trying to look something up in a library and you are not sure of the spelling. The hand-held dictionary/thesaurus can be very useful, but with a word of caution. Research (see Draffan and James 2006) found that the best hand-held dictionary for an adult dyslexic individual was that designed for children. The reason is that the more sophisticated ones offer too many alternative words, and this can be confusing. By cutting down the dictionary, the tool becomes more dyslexia-friendly.

Note that there are many types of dictionaries and thesauruses available for smart phones on the web at very low prices. Without doubt, the days of the stand-alone spellchecker and thesaurus are numbered but their usefulness remains. It is only their location that changes.

Scanners and optical character recognition (OCR)

Scanning is about the accurate reproduction of the printed word into an electronic format, and for the dyslexic individual it is a very important intermediate step to producing text in electronic format to be accessed by text-to-speech technology. The principles have been with us for many years and, while the changes in text-to-speech are coming rapidly, the changes to scanning are less obvious but happening nonetheless.

The results will depend upon:

1. the quality of the scanner;
2. the quality of the material being scanned;
3. the quality of the OCR software.

The quality of the scanner

The scanner is simply a method of capturing an electronic image of text at a resolution high enough for the OCR to make a good quality interpretation of the text. This can be achieved through a 'photocopier'-type machine (with appropriate software) which could take either the single page or a book on the imaging surface, through a small desktop-style flatbed scanner, through a dedicated desktop sheet-feed type scanner, or even through a standard digital camera.

Each of these has its own advantages, and there is little doubt that the main advances that one can expect to see in the next few years are to do with the convenient portable scanner – in other words, the camera built into the mobile phone. No longer will it be necessary to take the book to the photocopier, then the photocopy sheet to the scanner, and then use OCR. Instead we shall be able to photograph the book and send the image by email to an online OCR, which in turn is then sent to where we can use it. With everyday camera resolutions exceeding 10 mega pixels, resolution is no longer an issue. (However, you still need a fast connection between the phone and the internet if you have many pictures.)

Many users still try to make do with poor scans which suffer because the book could not be laid flat on the scanner. There are two solutions: (1) use a scanner that allows you to put the centre of the book on the edge of the scanner, and thereby produce a full-page scan with no distortion; or (2) use software that corrects poor scans. There are online services that will correct even a distorted low quality mobile phone image of a book: www.snapter. atiz.com/index.php

The quality of the material being scanned

Clearly the better the quality of the text, the better chance the software has of faithfully reproducing the text. A third-generation photocopy will have letters whose edges are degraded and it will have trouble correctly interpreting the results.

Also, if the source is a book, when you lay it on the photocopier, the image towards the centre of the book may be blurred or distorted. Without wanting to suggest that the backs of the books should be damaged, the flatter the book is on the scanner, the better will be the results.

The quality of the OCR software

With scanning, you get what you pay for. Dedicated scanning software, such as Omnipage will return very high levels of accuracy, even with degraded copies. Fonts and styles such as bold and italic will be retained, while layout will be faithfully reproduced. Some types put each paragraph into a separate text box, while others retain the original layout.

As the costs fall, so the amount of work you need to put in to make it a suitable document increases. In the end, you get what you pay for.

> ### Scanning tricks of the trade
>
> Sometimes the text from the reverse side of the page shows through and significantly interferes with the OCR. To overcome this, put a piece of black paper behind the page to be scanned. This will make the text on the reverse side disappear. The page will appear overall slightly darker, which can be compensated for by increasing the brightness and/or contrast.
>
> Also, if you use a camera to photograph a page, its software will try to compensate the exposure by thinking it is a typical scene. The consequence is that the image will appear grey. To overcome this, use the +/- (over-/under-) exposure control to get the optimum results. This is typically around +1.5 (over-exposed). (You will need to check your camera guide as to how to do this.)

Removing the 'carriage return' from a scanned Word document

Some OCR systems (especially some of the online ones) leave a carriage return at the end of each line if you have scanned a pdf into a Word document. This can be very annoying when you are trying to reformat text (though will not make too much difference if all you need to do is listen to the document). There is a trick to removing these 'in bulk', by using the Find and Replace function. However, it is most efficient if the document has a gap between each paragraph.

1. Go to Find and Replace >Replace and in the More drop-down menu, go to Special and Paragraph Mark. (This should appear as ^p.)
2. Put two Paragraph Marks in 'Find What', and 'XXXXX' in 'Replace with'. The use of 5 Xs is simply to make sure something is used that does not appear in the text.
3. Click Replace All.
4. Repeat the process, but using one Paragraph Mark, and replace it with a blank space (i.e. hit the space bar once).
5. Finally, put 'XXXXX' in 'Find What', and two Paragraph Marks in 'Replace with'.
6. If the document did not have gaps between the paragraphs, you can now simply add them back in.

OCR and handwriting

Handwriting recognition, whether it is on the smart phone, tablet pc or a dedicated 'pen' tool, is now common and fairly accurate. This accuracy can be assisted by the learning process of the software, which in turn will be dependent not upon the quality of the handwriting but on the consistency of the character writing. That is, no matter how bad you form a given letter, provided it is the same each time, the software will have a good chance of recognizing it (provided it is also distinct enough from another character).

Scanning hand-written notes is still a problem since the software used for the identification of handwriting on tablets and touch screens uses cues such as speed and direction, which is not available in a scan of notes. However, as touch screens become more widely available, we can expect to see greater use of this technology.

As well as the traditional flatbed scanner, there are several other types that are of use to the dyslexic individual, such as hand-held scanners or scanning pens.

Hand-held scanners

There are a number of different types and functions of hand-held scanners. In principle, these can be listed as the type that scans a page similar to a flatbed (e.g., the Docupen (www.planon.com) and the Superpen (www.emptech. info/product_details.php?ID=1836)). These can scan at the full width of the page, and claim to store up to 2,000 pages of text before needing to download. (This would be very dangerous, and regular downloads would be strongly recommended, no matter what the manufacturer claimed.)

Scanning pens

There are pens that are designed to provide immediate feedback, either as auditory feedback (i.e. it reads the word out loud), or by giving a definition (and reading the words). The three main types currently available are:

1. Quicklink Pen Elite
2. Scanning pen dictionary
3. Voice-Eye.

No doubt, others are in development, but the use of the mobile phone as a camera-based scanner seems to be the most logical future direction.

Mobile phones

The rapid development of mobile phones has enabled a lot of the standard tools used by the technology-empowered dyslexic individual (e.g., alarms, calendars and diaries) to be carried around in an ever-present piece of technology. Some of the more important functions are discussed in the box. With the technologies converging rapidly, it is difficult to predict future trends, especially in areas such as 'mobile' projectors (a projector built into the phone, powerful enough to project onto the wall in a darkened room). This suggests that the processing 'core' for the computer could be a 'mobile', and that the only additional requirement may be a suitable external keyboard.

Intellectual property rights (IPR)

It is important that at all times due respect is given to intellectual property rights (IPR). The significance of IPR to scanning is that you are entitled to photocopy no more than 5 per cent of any publication, and even then it must be for your own use. This means that even if there are several dyslexic individuals in the same course using the same book, each must scan the same pages for themselves. If one scan is shared, this breaks the IPR laws. This is true even if you own a copy of the book yourself, although publishers are less likely to bring the whole weight of the law down on you if you can prove it is only for your own use. But beware, there have been court cases over these issues, and it is always best to keep within the law.

Choosing a 'dyslexia-friendly' mobile phone

Whichever kind of phone you choose today, there will be a better one tomorrow, such is the nature and speed of development. However, when comparing mobile phones for use by the dyslexic individual, the following should be considered:

1. Ease of use – it is possible to configure most mobiles, if only you can read the manual. It is worth the effort to personalize and prioritize the keys. That is, where shortcuts are available to take you to the most useful functions, use them.
2. Easy access to a calendar and alarms – if they are not easy to reach, then you will not set them.
3. Loud alarms – a discreet, non-repeating alarm is of little use.
4. Good note-taking capabilities (e.g., through email) – these can be emailed to the main computer.
5. Uses a flash memory card – to export files, such as sound recording.
6. Has internet access – for those times when you need to check something you meant to check before you left home.
7. Has a built-in sound recorder – to take notes easily, including those made by others, such as a shopping list.
8. Has a built-in camera – in a car park, it is useful to take a picture of where you park the car, so you do not have to worry about forgetting where you left it. This can also be used for scanning.
9. GPS would be nice – for when you are not quite sure where you are or where you are going.
10. Easy-to-use sound system, for listening to e-books or music.

Author's Choice: I was fortunate in having an EU-funded project that used mobile phones, and so had an opportunity to compare them all. I held onto my Nokia N70 for over five years as it bounced well when dropped, as well as having most functions (except sound recording). I replaced it with a Nokia N95, again at the time the top-of-the-range device with the key areas covered.

I also had the opportunity to compare the BlackBerry and iPhone. In my opinion, the BlackBerry is a wonderful business tool which is perfect for my work. If I wanted a tool that had lots of distracting applications that had little value, I would choose an iPhone.

Using digital phone cameras

Although the camera is not currently seen as a piece of assistive hardware that is used by dyslexic individuals, there are times when they can be useful, especially when built into a mobile phone. Of course, the 'pictures' can be used for effective note-taking tool for later 'transcribing' or inclusion in some form of presentation. However, as noted above, improved resolution means they have the potential to rival the traditional scanner as a piece of technology that can be used to change print into e-text and even spoken text. One example of an alternative to traditional scanning is www.scanr.com. By taking a picture of a full A4 page of text using a traditional high-end (5 meg pixel) phone camera, you can send it to that address and then view the result on the website.

Talking text on mobiles

There are now phones with built-in technology that allows you to take a picture of text, and it will read it back to you. No doubt this will become more widespread in the next few years, as will the logical extension of using the 'webcam' built into the laptop as the scanning tool.

Parking problems

Ever lost your car in a car park, maybe when shopping or on holiday? A simple way to remember where you parked is to take a photo of your car in position. Simply stand well back so you can see plenty of landmarks around, put your car in the middle, and shoot. Then you can just look at the picture later (or show a policeman!), provided you remembered not to delete it.

Talking clocks and alarms on a smart phone

Memory problems and time keeping are major issues for the dyslexic individual. It is easy for the parents to develop systems to remind the dyslexic child what to do and when to do it, by using simple strategies such as a paper-based timetable at the front door. But when they leave home, independent adults need to self-manage their time and actions. At first glance, talking clocks and alarms seem to be an ideal solution. But there is a problem with those – you need to remember to set them and then remember what they are trying to remind you about.

So the stand-alone device which simply makes a noise may be useful to tell you to stop what you are doing but, unless you have a routine that says 'look in your diary to see what the alarm is for', the danger is that the device will simply be turned off and the 'activity' ignored. And you will forget to do what you set the alarm to remind you to do. Therefore, at the very least, you need a way to match the alarm with the reason it went off.

The smart phone is now able to provide the alarm, and a place to say what the reminder is for. Like all systems, the trick is to get used to using it, and making its use easy. For example, rather than search through a series of menus, use shortcuts to arrive quickly at the screen you want.

If the phone is the chosen way to organize one's diary, there is still a matter of choosing the right software, and synchronizing it with other systems, such as online organizers and task managers. The biggest problem is that there are over 100 task manager systems to recommend and everybody has their own preference. (See http://technodys.blogspot.com for suggestions.)

Case study 3 Paul's routine

Paul was supervised by his parents every day at primary school. His bag was packed, the right books and sports shoes put in place, pencil case (with a place for everything, and everything in its own place, so he could see when something was missing) plus bus pass (attached to a ski pass chain to avoid being lost) and money for a snack if needed, or to buy a pen when one was lost. For secondary school, they bought him a PDA (later updated to a smart phone), knowing that at some point he would lose it but also attached to a ski pass chain, with the understanding that if he lost it, it was because he had broken the rules and removed the phone from the chain, and therefore had to buy a replacement with his 'allowance'. Needless to say, it was never lost! The phone also had his name and address scratched on the outside, and inside, plus a ICED number (see box on p. 93). The routine was that at breakfast the list of entries for the rest of the week were checked (pack kit, parties, regular school activities, school trips, etc.) and new ones entered. An alarm would be set at an appropriate time for each, and usually more than one alarm, e.g. the school trip alarm went off the night before, and before breakfast. Missed, ignored or forgotten alarms were 'remembered' by having the routine of checking the list at breakfast. This routine was reinforced daily (with varying degrees of success) but after four years became a regular and acceptable way to avoid missing (most) activities. And at university the system was admired and copied.

Note-taking pens

There are several types of note-taking aids which work on two basic principles:

1. They use a location device to track the position of the pen 'nib'.
2. They use special paper which has positional information.

The principle is that the movement of the pen is transferred to the computer and can be stored either in the original format, or (if legible) can be saved as text using OCR.

The first type has the advantage of not requiring special paper, but is very sensitive to any movement of the paper as you write. The second (e.g., Livescribe) uses reasonably inexpensive special paper that provides locational-sensitive data.

These pens may also include voice recording, although the occasions when the individual can talk out loud to the pen may be limited. However, it does allow synchronization between the conversation and the note taking. If this could be extended so that a remote mike could be used in collaboration with the pen, this would make it more effective for the dyslexic user. Initial research findings in Sweden show this to be a very useful tool for dyslexic individuals.

Talking calculator

Although they may appear to be a gimmick, there are some dyslexic individuals who find it a lot easier to hear mathematical results from a calculator. There are several types around that can easily be bought on the internet, including those that can be installed on a mobile phone. However, there are also several online versions, which remove the need of having a stand-alone version. Interestingly, many shops in China use talking calculators to tell their clients how much to pay. However, in this case the issue is usually one of illiteracy rather than dyslexia or dyscalculia.

Headphones

The choice of headphones is very personal. Some people prefer those that go into the ear, others prefer ones that sit on the ear, and some prefer the type that covers the ear. Obviously cost is an important factor, but, if there is an option, then the 'noise reduction' type, which creates an 'anti-noise' to reduce background sound, is preferable. The recent advances in noise reduction (and wider acceptance especially for aircraft travel) make this type of headphone very affordable, and a boon for the dyslexic individual who would prefer to cut out as much background noise as possible. (There is plenty of research that suggests dyslexic individuals have problems separating out the important sounds from background noise.) But there are issues with different types, with the biggest problem being what happens when the battery runs out. The problems are that at least one manufacturer uses internal rechargeable batteries (i.e. you cannot access them to replace them but have to plug in the charger). Unfortunately, when the batteries discharge in this type, sound is lost. With others of similar quality, when the batteries fail you can at least still hear the sound. For the dyslexic individual, the need to remember to check battery charge may be a deciding factor against a particular model.

Directional GPS guide

The theory is simple – dyslexic individuals have difficulty with directions and map reading. Therefore, a device that can identify where the user is, and in which direction he or she should go, should be a boon. But it seems a bit like a spellchecker that offers ten alternatives – you still have to be able to read all of them, know their different meanings, and then decide. The GPS guide is made for those who need to know all the details but do not necessarily have problems with left and right, and following maps. In some exceptional cases it may be worth considering. But for many dyslexic individuals it could present more problems than it would solve.

Increasingly there are a number of software-led solutions that utilize the GPS of the smart phone, such as Google Latitude and Zhiing. These allow users to find out where they are, and to advise others how to find them. There is little doubt that these services will become mainstream, and be of considerable benefit to the dyslexic user, provided, that is, that the instructions are clear!

Creativity in Japan

In Japan, when dyslexic individuals get lost, they often take out their mobile phone, take a photo, send it to a friend and say 'Where am I?' This is a creative solution to an age-old problem.

Conclusion: in future

The speed of development of the technology is so fast that to speculate about the future now may be dangerous, but some directions are clear. More than 15 years ago, Larry Ellison (CEO of Oracle) argued with Bill Gates (Microsoft) that in the future software would run through the web, and that the computer would be 'dumb', not needing to hold software locally. This vision is now beginning to appear, with the result that hardware has less to do. As a consequence, the technology specifications may well change rapidly in the coming years, as needs shift.

With respect to the hardware itself, there is already a blurring of the distinction between devices, as laptops, sub-notebooks and mobile phones begin to run the same software, and this is inevitable as operating systems begin to become common across the diverse hardware. It is not hard to envisage a future whereby the keyboard folds into a pocket (already possible) with the processing power built into it. The screen rolls up (small versions already used for e-books), and the device could be used with the built-in projector (already available), or hooked up to a large screen. Fast internet connection gives rapid access to online software. And the phone is used via a small headset.

As the technology continues to become more portable, the issue in the future for the dyslexic user is to discern how the functionality can be optimized and made dyslexia-friendly without a loss of functionality or portability.

4 Assistive Software

Introduction

Assistive software has made considerable progress in the past few years as the impact of Web 2 technologies and its acceptance become more widespread. This has allowed us to escape the confines of the traditional 'big three' of text-to-speech, speech-to-text and concept mapping. However, there is still little mapping between what is feasible and what is useful, let alone making needs analysis evidence based.

This chapter will start with a theoretical framework that identifies the specific issues as highlighted in previous chapters and maps them to what can be achieved. However, in doing so, it looks beyond the traditional access to education normally highlighted in such reviews, to encompass 'life skills' including accessing the internet for business and leisure, and using memory aids.

Dyslexic individuals, irrespective of whether they are at school, college, university or in work, will be 'receiving' large amounts of information through the spoken and written word. That is, they are receiving other people's thoughts and ideas. The spoken word could be through lessons, lectures or conversations. It could also be as a sound file such as a podcast or even as video. The written word may be printed media, such as books, magazines, newspapers or single sheets of paper, or it could be electronic media such as a Word document, internet text or other similar format. In all cases, the role of the assistive technology is to make the material more accessible, to assist in accessing the meaning of the content in a more appropriate format.

In the past, it tended to be the case that a piece of technology, either software or hardware, became available and somebody realized that it might be useful for the dyslexic individual as well as, say, for the ⟹

blind. This was certainly the case with text-to-speech, while concept mapping first appeared in the commercial sector. Unfortunately, little attempt has been made to develop any form of theoretical model, mapping the technology to the needs of the individual. This leads not only to *ad hoc* development of technology but also specifications for support are based on what is available (or even worse, only what is known by the specifier) and not what is required. Therefore, before we look at individual components, we need to understand the relationship between the processes and the technology.

Mapping technology to the reading process

Figure 4.1 presents the relationship between the components involved in the reading process and the technology that could assist access to its contents. In brief, in order to take advantage of the technology, the material needs to be in an electronic format. A paper book can be scanned and, with the aid of optical character recognition (OCR), can be accessed as an e-document. Once in this format, you can use text-to-speech to listen to it, summarizers to reduce the number of words to read it, and preferences to ease eye strain (more extensively covered in Chapter 6). Sound recording (e.g., either recording from text-to-speech, or recording the human voice) is also a useful tool to aid revision and comprehension.

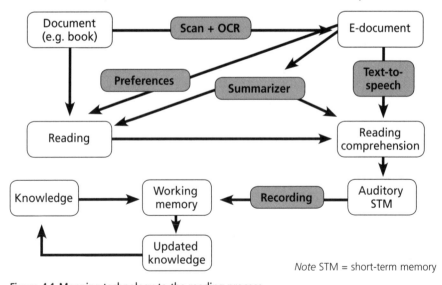

Note STM = short-term memory

Figure 4.1 Mapping technology to the reading process

Mapping technology to the writing process

Figure 4.2 shows the main relationships between the technology and processes involved in writing. The transfer of thought to paper involves pulling knowledge from the diverse parts of the brain, putting it into a cohesive format using working memory (as well as the executive functioning and other processes) to create an output. This may be verbalized directly or can be in the form of a concept map for brainstorming before committing to writing. Speech-to-text may be used to turn the spoken word into the written format. The word processor provides validation, which can include spelling and grammar checking. Validation may also include listening to the text through text-to-speech (to ensure that what is written down is what was intended).

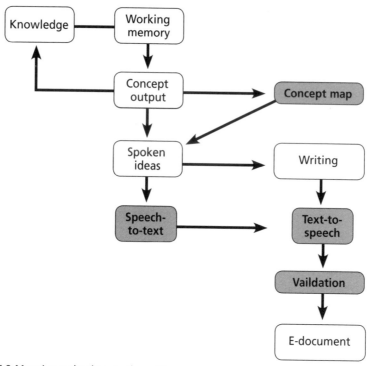

Figure 4.2 Mapping technology to the writing process

Having identified the main components, we need to look at them in detail, starting with the most widely used and understood: text-to-speech, speech-to-text and concept mapping.

Text-to-speech (TTS)

Put simply, text-to-speech (TTS) allows the person who is receiving information in electronic format to access it through the auditory channel rather than having to read the text visually. That is, he or she can understand the text without having to decode the words on the page. Clearly this offers substantial advantages to the dyslexic individual in many circumstances, and is usually the piece of software that is central to dyslexia support. However, in order to maximize its potential, we need to have a basic understanding of the technology, its strengths and limitations, and the diverse ways in which it can also be used. Furthermore, if we know what is available, we can make informed choices about what to use and under what circumstances.

Terminology

There is much debate over the term one should use for software (or the processes) that takes the written word and turns it into an auditory presentation. The two most common terms are 'text-to-speech' and 'screenreader'. The differences are technical, and to some extent are a product of history. It is about whether the software accesses the video card, or if it is an automated system that does not even have a visual interface (e.g., an automated telephone system that uses text files rather than pre-recorded voices). Now other terms are starting to be introduced, such as 'talking wordbar'. Recently, a number of websites have been developed that have the ability to extract text from pictures on the screen, thereby making it even more confusing for those who prefer to use the term 'screenreader'. However, in this book, the term 'text-to-speech' is used, since everybody knows what it means in the context of dyslexia.

Text-to-speech software is often one of the first types of assistive software the dyslexic individual will encounter. There are many types, as will be discussed later in this chapter. Within the context of the framework we need to appreciate that TTS changes the electronic document into a sound presentation or sound file.

Uses of text-to-speech software

There are many ways in which text-to-speech software can be used. It can read:

- an electronic document (e.g., in Microsoft Word or a pdf)
- web pages
- email and chat.

It can also be used as a tool to do the following:

- listen to other people's words
- proofread one's own work
- check the correct pronunciation of a word or phrase
- reduce eye strain caused by excessive reading, such as preparing for examinations
- listen to text while doing other tasks, such as travelling
- assist study or access a second language.

Principles behind text-to-speech software

It is not necessary to know all the technical details of how text-to-speech software works in order to make it effective. However, it is useful to know the principles, since it helps us understand why it can sometimes go wrong.

In principle, the techniques involve joining parts of speech together, such as individual phones, diphones and half-phones, and using pre-recorded speech. This joining method (sometimes referred to as concatenative synthesis) means that it can make new and 'unfamiliar' words, and does not have to rely on an extensive dictionary. Diphone synthesis joins sounds in what is best described as using the middle part of a pair of phonemes. This allows a smooth transition between sounds. This is now the most common type. The pre-recorded type is for fixed situations (e.g., train announcements) and is sometimes used for text-to-speech where a concatenative system is not available. However, it requires the availability of a sound file for each word. Although far from ideal, these can be better than nothing and a lifesaver for many dyslexic individuals.

In recent years, the drive has been toward more 'human-like' sound quality, with better intonation and greater 'fluency'. This requires analysis of larger unit size, to identify possible use of word combinations, and how the word is being used (e.g., is the word 'bow' used as a noun or verb?). Although this is better for non-dyslexic users, ironically there is anecdotal evidence to suggest that some dyslexic individuals prefer the more staccato voice, where each word is separately pronounced.

Categories of text-to-speech

In the early days of text-to-speech (which was then mostly used by the blind or partially sighted community), few kinds of software were available, and there was little need to consider the categories. However, the types and uses have rapidly expanded, so that now we need to carefully consider the context. Needless to say, the more expensive software versions can handle most of the diverse conditions which we now encounter, including reading the stand-alone document, email and the web. However, it is also good to know what else is available.

Although it is not easy to categorize all text-to-speech software, it is worth considering the types that are available, since they may be important in the implementation of a needs analysis development of a support program, and in accessibility of websites, e-learning and general content delivery. There is little doubt new forms of text-to-speech, that currently are not even in development will appear in future. The technology and concepts are moving fast. Note that although these are set out as if they are independent categories, frequently they are integrated with other software.

The classic (toolbar type)

The classic version of text-to-speech software is a stand-alone version that sits in your computer. It works using a toolbar, and works with any software, including Microsoft Word, email and the Web. This toolbar can be at the top of the screen or floating. The controls include stop and play, speech change and alternative voices, and, depending on the price, may have options such as the ability to highlight words or sentences as they are spoken. These are often integrated with tools such as spellcheckers and word prediction, or help with homophones. Commercial examples include TextHelp and ClaroRead.

Stand-alone cut and paste TTS

Some stand-alone versions of text-to-speech allow the user to copy the text from a document or webpage and paste it into the text box. From there, it can then be read. Probably the best-known free version is Readplease (www. readplease.com), although that company also has commercial versions. Options include different voices, highlighting as the text is spoken, and changes to speed and font size. The voice quality will depend on the version, with commercial versions providing superior quality and added functionality.

Online cut and paste TTS

An increasing number of websites provide text boxes for inserting one's own text, similar to the offline versions. Most are fairly standard, but some include speaking avatars (a talking head). One example is to be found at www.imtranslator.com. That has the option to read English, Spanish, French, German, Italian, Brazilian Portuguese, Korean, Japanese, Chinese and Russian. (It also offers translations – see Chapter 8 for more details.)

Talking word processors

Despite the rise of the stand-alone do-everything toolbar, there are still a number of dedicated talking word processors on the market. These integrated packages are mostly aimed at children and blind or partially sighted users. They have the advantage of working seamlessly with the word processor, and ensure the user keeps on task.

Talking word processors – online

At the time of writing, there are no known online talking word processors. However, there is little doubt that mash-up techniques will bring these technologies together soon, and we shall see text-to-speech appearing in new sites or in the likes of Google Docs and Zoho.

Talking web browser

A number of talking web browsers have been created, especially for the visually impaired community. However, more recently the approach has been to provide add-ons to existing browsers. One example is VoxFox for the Mozilla Firefox browsers.

Embedded talking tools – webpage based

A number of companies produce tools that can be embedded within the webpage by the webmaster. These are used by specialist dyslexia sites to ensure they are compliant with the needs of their primary users, thereby promoting an inclusive approach. There are two variants of this: (1) to use the tool that is entirely on the site; or (2) to download a small associated program that works with their websites. Examples include Talklets and Browsealoud.

Another example of embedded tools that work at the single-word level is AnswerTips. Unlike the other embedded tools, with this tool you can double click on a single word and the user is provided with a definition and pronunciation guide as well as the spoken word. This approach is sometimes referred to as *glossing*, and has been shown to aid reading comprehension for those with limited reading skills, such as the dyslexic individual and the reader of English as an additional language (e.g., Ko 2005). For a good example of this dyslexia-friendly method, try Aesop's Fables at www.aesopfables.com or the TechnoDys blog (http://technodys.blogspot.com).

Embedded talking tools – Adobe Read Out Loud

Some software has its own built-in accessible software, of which the most widely available (although little known) version is Adobe Read Out Loud, built into the freely available Acrobat Reader. This means that you can ask the program to read any pdf to you without needing to install separate software. It uses the voices built into the computer and, although these voices may not be as good as the commercial text-to-speech engines, it is a very useful tool if you have no alternative installed. It is accessible in Acrobat through View > Read Out Loud.

Commercial versus free software

The old expression is you get what you pay for. So if software is free, does that mean it is worth nothing? And if it is so good, why don't more people use it and why buy the commercial software? Let's consider two main free software packages: concept mapping and text-to-speech.

Text-to-speech (TTS) is a little different. What the additional money pays for is the quality of the voice. Free TTS uses free Microsoft voices; commercial programs use commercial voices. These are more 'human'-like with better sound for each word, better sound 'rhythms' in sentences, and better ability to handle headings, bullet points, etc. The other advantage is that they tend to be in the form of toolbars which work with all programs, rather than having to change between programs.

Concept mapping in principle is a relatively straightforward program, as the introduction of several online versions have recently shown. However, it is the details that count. For example, Inspiration and Kidspiration have huge picture libraries. MindFull is not alone in having sound recording, but is a low cost solution that is included in this (dyslexia-friendly) option. Some people talk about the advantages of different layout. But that is minor and, if they wanted to and made a commercial difference, developers could allow users to change the layout mode. It is likely that online collaborative concept mapping will be more important in future, possibly with the emergence of remote tutoring. Many of these are currently free for low usage, and you pay for the more advanced service. Furthermore, at least one commercial concept mapping software producer has already launched an online version of its software.

$\Rightarrow$

So, as always, it depends on the use. If it is just a very basic requirement, where the user wants to experiment or is waiting for funding, then he or she can try the free versions. If you need quality and support, and you have a budget, then invest in the commercial software.

An additional factor to consider is the level of support. Freeware has no support. However, all the major manufacturers have help desks to support those with installation difficulties, including many dyslexic individuals. This is not because dyslexic individuals cannot use the product, but because (as is obvious!) the manual is a written document, and the purpose of the software is to access the written word! A classic Catch-22 situation.

File uploading

There are a number of websites that provide a service that allows you to upload a file and have the text spoken. These sites also usually allow an mp3 file to be downloaded. Some also display the text for reading on screen. Examples include www.ispeech.com and www.spokentext.com. The latter is also available in Spanish and French.

Special readers

Website readers

There are many services that now allow you to enter a website address and the text is read back. However, not all of them successfully manage the layout issues.

Blog readers

There are a number of dedicated blog reading services. One example of a specialist service is Blogbard (www.blogbard.com) which reads the blog entry-by-entry. It is also possible with some of these readers to embed the code in the blog and have it read directly.

Mobile text-to-speech

Text-to-speech has been available on the mobile phone for many years, but it is only with the advent of the smart phone, and increased processing power and storage capacity that mainstream phones have the potential to fully exploit text-to-speech. For example, Nokia now has free downloads for certain phones (http://europe.nokia.com/A4286225).

Outputs

Although 'outputs' are implicit to text-to-speech, it is worth considering the two types, which are 'live' sound, and recorded and saved sound. The wide use of mobile phones with mp3 player capability has (arguably) led to a surge in the availability of software that will provide a file that can be played away from the computer. This will allow people to listen to their text on the bus, on the train, in the car, etc.

However, the downside is that you need a good auditory memory, since you cannot easily return to the same place. For example, if you had saved this chapter to an mp3, most people would do it as one file. This means returning to a given section is problematic. To be most effective, the recording needs to be managed. In this case, it may be preferable to record each section separately. No doubt improved tagging of sound will be included in future developments.

How to check your text-to-speech software

Use the following text to test your text-to-speech software. You can find it at www.wdnf. info/testingtts. This text is designed to be awkward for text-to-speech software to read without errors. The key areas of difficulty are:

- bullet points
- headers
- homonyms
- intonation.

Bullet points and headers can run into the next line if there is no full stop at the end. Although we can clearly see what must be a header or bullet point in text, even if it is in a language we are not familiar with, some software packages do not recognize this.

Homonyms are words that are spelled the same but are pronounced differently. Most people do not have problems with sentences such as:

1. He wanted to present a present to her.
2. The cow was too close to close the gate.
3. The wind blew too hard to wind in the sail.

Clearly the words are common, and the software identifies the parts of speech and therefore probable pronunciation of each occurrence of the word.

However, the following were more problematic for some but not all the software tested:

1. Just for a minute, it looked minute.
2. A new bandage was wound around the wound.
3. His insurance was invalid because he was an invalid.
4. He could not bow as he held his bow. So he put down his bow and arrow. Then he could bow to the king.
5. As she thought she saw the tear in her dress, she shed a tear. Then she saw she did not tear her dress, so she shed another tear.

Adjusting parameters of TTS

Text-to-speech software can come with a variety of voices, with the quality depending on the price paid. Microsoft developed a series of voices that are freely available and are exploited by freeware. Higher quality voices are expensive to produce, and the range of languages available is limited, although continuously expanding with a strong demand from the blind and partially sighted communities.

Before opting for the expensive versions, there is anecdotal evidence that suggests the older system which has small pauses between words, and less intonation, may be preferable for the dyslexic individual. This is because it gives slightly longer to absorb the information. Hence some developers are now including the option of a pause between words. This is not the same as adjusting speed, which has the words spoken faster without changing the pitch.

Clearly TTS has moved forward considerably in the past ten years, from a monotone that could be used with few programs to sophisticated human-like voices and usable in many contacts. We can expect to see in the future an even greater use of context-dependent text. For example, at the bus stop, information may be spoken by the mobile with the information available through Bluetooth, location-dependent or by taking a photo of it.

Speech-to-text

Text-to-speech is about listening to what others have produced. Speech-to-text is about producing one's own work. Speech-to-text software gives the capability to turn the spoken word into flowing text. It has advanced considerably in recent years to provide high levels of accuracy with little training, and has made essay and report writing much easier for many dyslexic individuals.

No longer do you need to pause between words. And even strong accents and dialects are no barrier to its use. Yes, an extended training period may be required. But since this is now as little as ten minutes (or nothing if you want to train it as you go), the additional training for accents is minimal.

This technology provides the dyslexic users with the freedom to write what they like, and can put the text into any document either directly or through cut and paste. When the software does not recognize a word, the user is presented with options to choose the correct word. This can be problematic as you need to understand the difference between the alternatives but, with speech-to-text and dictionary options, the additional stress is minimized. The speech-to-text also allows the software to read back what has been written, providing the first level of proofreading.

Speech-to-text services on the phone

There are already speech-to-text services on mobile phones such as voice search with Google. Given that the quality is already very high, it does not take much to imagine that soon we shall have speech-to-text on a mobile phone, where the main (processing-heavy) work is carried out on remote servers.

Microphone quality

The quality is clearly affected by the microphone used, and the context. For an individual dictating his or her own work into a headset in a quiet environment, the ability to reproduce the words should be very high.

Digital dictation machines are also a useful tool, allowing the user to record notes and essays away from the computer. However, the quality is improved if a good quality lapel mike is used instead of the built-in microphone.

Voice quality and recording others

The software will only work well for a voice that it has been trained on. This means that using it in a lecture hall for a one-off event is unlikely to provide rewarding results. If the recorder can be at the front, quality may be improved, but not enough for speech-to-text. However, if the person speaking is a regular speaker (e.g., a lecturer providing a lecture once a week for a term), it may be possible to gain permission to attach the recorder and mike to the person ensuring high quality, and then set up a second voice file on the software specially for that lecturer. If there are several lectures, there may be a good opportunity to have good quality lecture notes.

It is not so far to move to the next step, which is full internet-based speech-to-text. However, the quantity of data to be transferred is enormous, and it is a big leap from working with intranets and internal networks to moving onto the internet. However, development of appropriate data packaging techniques, some local processing and faster transmission speeds together offer the potential to eventually use the internet for speech-to-text.

Does assistive technology encourage children not to learn the basics?

Some people have suggested that by introducing, for example, speech-to-text to seven-year-olds, it will take away the incentive to learn literacy skills. But who would take away a wheelchair from somebody with poor motor skills even if in the long term he or she may be able to walk again? The answer is matching the support to the needs. Most dyslexic individuals become frustrated and demotivated because they cannot do the same work as their peers. If a child cannot access information in a book, is it not better to provide him or her with support that can overcome that difficulty? A child who is two years behind on his or her reading will have trouble keeping up with classwork if he or she cannot access what others read. To delay support will simply push him or her further behind with respect to his or her knowledge. Similarly, with speech-to-text – if this is used appropriately in conjunction with learning phonics, then the child will have a chance to fulfil his or her potential. To spend an hour trying to write an essay by hand which produces just one or two sentences will be less productive than a combination of 30 minutes of speech-to-text and 30 minutes of phonics instruction related to what was written.

Typing

Technically it may be suggested that typing is a learned skill and not assistive technology. However, it would seem legitimate to cover it here since, although it is a skill learned and the software is subsequently discarded, the software may also be described as that which may open up literacy as a productive process to many dyslexic individuals.

Although there is a lack of evidence to prove it, acquisition of efficient typing skills can help improve spelling. The logic is that we learn the key (and motor) combinations of the more common words, and this helps ensure the spelling is correct. Hence, as suggested above, its inclusion in many computer-based phonics programs. This is because the memory becomes motor-based rather than sound–letter correspondence-based. The evidence for this is that touch typists often do not have to think about what they type, and can sometimes hold a conversation about a different topic as they type perfectly. However, the dyslexic individual will also need more practice to acquire the skills than the non-dyslexic individual. There are a number of typing tutors available that are well suited to the dyslexic learner, since they use phonics principles to teach typing skills.

Over the past ten years many people have highlighted the advantages of using the computer for the preparation of work. Put simply, most dyslexic individuals can hide their differences when using the computer since their work does not have the 'style' signs in presentation that reveal their difficulties.

However, comparatively little attention has been paid to the development of keyboarding skills for dyslexic users except within a few computer-based phonics programs. Why? What would be the impact of improved typing skills? The answer lies mostly in the lack of understanding of the advantages of touch typing among those who teach dyslexic learners. However, there are problems, not least of which is that the dyslexic individual will have greater problems than most in learning typing skills. This is for two reasons: (1) because the spelling is more problematic, there will be greater hesitancy; and (2) frequently motor skill difficulties come with dyslexia, meaning that the development of these motor engrams is slower. But they will still form.

The 'speed' of typing will ultimately be a trade-off between the speed of the keystrokes and accuracy. A person employed specifically for his or her typing skills will be able to listen to a sound file and type, without ever needing to look at the screen. How can people do this? Because they are able to distinguish the words clearly, know the spelling, and know the finger combinations to type that word error-free. Interestingly, there is evidence that suggests that the brain remembers keystroke combinations. We develop what are called motor engrams – a combination of motor skills that follow each other. So, the combination 'ight' (as in 'night' and 'light') becomes automated, rather than having to consider each letter in turn. Ultimately, if you can get the right typing program that will teach you phonics and how to type at the same time, the systems of motor, visual and sound will all reinforce each other. Therefore, even without spellcheckers, spelling can become better when you learn to type.

One of the problems for all new typists, but especially so for dyslexic typists, is confidence. Most learners will accept that they will make errors. The principle of touch typing is that one's fingers sit over the keys in the centre of the keyboard, with the index fingers over 'f' and 'j'. (Usually these keys have a small ridge on them to help verify correct finger placement.) The typist should then be watching the screen all the time and not keep looking down at the keyboard. Users will learn where the keys are, and slowly improve their skills, accepting the errors on the way. However, many dyslexic typists will have greater difficulty remembering where the keys are, and therefore will want to repeatedly look down at the keyboard before pushing the keys. Although this happens with everybody, it tends to persist more with dyslexic individuals. While it can still lead to a very effective typing speed, obviously the more automated it is, the better it will be. It is for this reason that due consideration should be given to the type of program used, for, although a 'phonics' approach may seem a logical choice, the program with keystroke repetition should also be considered for some. Examples of phonics and typing programs include Nessy Fingers and Touch Type Read and Spell. You can find many others listed at www.typingsoft.com/all_typing_tutors.htm.

 Author's Choice: Qwerty Warriorz. I am a touch typist but if I want to have fun and check my skills, this is great. It may also be good for reluctant typists as it is a 'shoot 'em up' game where you have little choice but to use touch typing. Just look it up on Google!

Auto correction

Another potential problem that does not necessarily disappear is the lack of coordination. Consider a simple word to type such as 'the'. This requires a combination of keystroke that uses the left hand, then right, then left again. The problem is that many dyslexic users will have a sequencing problem, with the consequence that they type left, left, right, ending up with 'teh'. Fortunately, programs such as Word have an auto correction section (Tools/Autocorrect Options). This allows the entry of a wrong spelling to be automatically replaced by the correct spelling. Thus, 'eth' is also auto-corrected. This facility can be used for any regularly misspelled word and is far quicker and simpler than trying to notice the error and replace it.

Sat navs

Various research has been done on dyslexia and driving but none so far on dyslexia and using satellite navigation systems. However, there are a number of issues that are worthy of consideration when discussing 'sat navs' and related devices. However, it is important to stress, as in all cases, that every individual is different, and even if as a group there may be problems, it does not mean that a specific person will have problems. Indeed, many dyslexic individual find them a real lifesaver, and now cannot imagine life without them. Furthermore, you do not have to be dyslexic to have problems with sat navs. The problems are not specific to the dyslexic individual, but are related to cognitive demands.

Online location services

The recent launch of online location services that can be accessed through the mobile phone also adds a new dimension. These include Google Latitude and Zhiing, which have features such as being able to send information to a friend (or taxi driver) to tell him or her where to find you. While they do not currently have text-to-speech, they will no doubt enable those features in the near future.

Synthesis and summarizer software

When people think about cutting down the stress in reading a long document, usually the first thought is to use text-to-speech. However, there is an alternative, which is to cut down the amount of text (and then maybe use text-to-speech). Improved data analysis techniques have led to the development of a number of very sophisticated pieces of software that provide managers with the ability to sift through reports quickly. Commercial versions include Copernic and Intellexer.

There are a number of free ones on the internet of variable quality. However, there is also a version built into Microsoft Word. Like the commercial version, Word allows you to specify how much you want to cut out, and if you want to highlight key points, insert an executive summary (with or without the original) or create a new document.

Testing Microsoft Word AutoSummarize

I used the AutoSummarize in Microsoft Word with its default (25 per cent) settings on the section in the Preface entitled 'Guide to the Chapters'. It has reduced the text from 1,473 to 376 words. You may like to compare this below with the original. Most of the key points are here.

How can you talk about supporting the dyslexic individual if you are not sure what dyslexia is? Sadly no such other text exists.

The rest of this book is dedicated to the technology and how it can be used.

Where possible, research is presented in the relevant chapters of this book, which will at least offer some comfort to those trying to make logical choices.

There are two main areas for testing with respect to the dyslexic individual – testing of skills and abilities and the testing of knowledge. Chapter 2 is concerned with skills testing, with particular respect to the underlying difficulties characteristic of the difficulties of a dyslexic individual. This includes literacy difficulties and underlying cognitive difficulties.

Chapter 3 concentrates on the assistive hardware that currently exists to help the dyslexic individual. The chapter looks at specialist hardware as well as providing an overview of the main components that will allow informed choices to be made.

The chapter on assistive software, Chapter 4, analyses both text-to-speech and speech-to-text technology and discusses concept mapping.

Chapter 5 presents software with respect to the defining characteristic of dyslexic individuals: literacy acquisition. This chapter looks at the different skills that can be taught, and the research to back up the claims of technology.

Chapter 6 attempts to pull together the diverse strands that impact upon the user interface. Usability, including interface design, readability as well as the need to ensure content can be used in conjunction with text-to-speech.

E-learning and technology-led knowledge assessments are predicted to be pervasive in education. Chapter 7 provides a background to the implications of e-learning for dyslexic individuals.

Chapter 8 looks at multilingualism in relation to dyslexia and how technology can play a key role in the support of these individuals, whether they are Welsh first language speakers, Chinese speakers in Manchester or Bulgarian dyslexic students in London.

Chapter 9 attempts to delineate what have been the barriers to progress to date, and how change will happen.

Concept mapping

Concept mapping was developed by Joseph Novak in the 1970s at Cornell University as a way to help students understand the relationship between concepts. Concept maps have been used for many years in the field of dyslexia as a useful tool to begin the process of developing a framework for a project, essay or other area that needs a clear structure.

Concept mapping software (sometimes referred to as mind mapping) is a useful tool to brainstorm ideas and provide a focal point from which essays and projects can be developed. It allows all the ideas to be mapped out, and the relationships between ideas to be established. This is where dyslexic individuals can use their creative skills and their strengths in basic knowledge to overcome their writing difficulties. Using a combination of linked images, ideas and concepts, dyslexic students can map out ideas with keywords and pictures that can often convey as much as a long essay. However, they are not restricted in their use, and examples include the following:

- to help memorize data for learning and exams
- to develop and plan essays and theses
- to draft presentations
- to plan projects and easily explain them to others
- to brainstorm ideas
- to help develop projects.

These can be used in two ways, either as a way to brainstorm, whereby all the thoughts are put down onto the paper (or screen) first and then the links established. Alternatively you can start with the central structure in the middle, and build outwards. The former is easiest when the space is unrestricted (such as with paper on a table or when using two screens) while the latter is most convenient when a small screen is used. Clearly, if you have a small screen, it is possible to use techniques such as layers and swapping between pages. But that requires more visual memory and is not suitable for all dyslexic individuals.

The computerized version of concept maps has many advantages over the 'old-fashioned' paper-based versions, since they can be 'clean' (i.e. all the errors are hidden) and they can be colourful, easily saved and modified. Furthermore, the change to view examples, to access libraries and be provided with all the diverse tools can be empowering. However, most teachers of dyslexic individuals would still advocate learning the basics through making a paper-based version before attempting to make computer-based concept maps. The reason is that there is little that can beat (or can recreate) the physical act of putting down one's ideas on lots of scraps of paper, covering a table top and then trying to organize them. This can be far more empowering than trying to squeeze everything into a small screen. This idea of unlimited space should be seen as the starting point of development of maps, with the computerized version following once the basics are in place. Unfortunately the limited space on the computer screen, particularly with webbooks and netbooks, rarely allows enough space to truly brainstorm the ideas before they are organized. Zoom options software and dual screen technique both offer a technological solution, but both have their limitations.

Mind map or concept map?

The terms 'mind map' and 'concept map' are both defined as being methods of visual representation of ideas and their relationships. It may be argued that the main difference is that the mind map has a single core idea from which all others radiate, whereas the concept map shows the relationships and need not have a core. Thus a mind map may be seen as a concept map that radiates from a single idea.

The concept map is said to have originated with Novak in the 1970s, and was developed to help science students understand the complex relationship between diverse concepts. The popularization of the mind map was through the work of Tony Buzan. The term 'Mind Maps™' was registered as a trademark in 1990 in both the UK and USA by Buzan.

Although this software was originally developed with the commercial sector in mind, these tools are now integrated into mainstream education, although their uptake is largely dependent upon the enthusiasm of the individual teacher. The commercial sector has integrated its concepts into diverse areas of work management, from project conceptualization to workflow. The basic tools have become more sophisticated with the increase in software, the drive for differentiation of software in the marketplace, and the demands of the user. Although there are still some visual differences, these tend to be cosmetic and are related to trying to suggest a different (superior) use for the marketplace. However, in reality, functionality is very similar, with each copying the 'advantages' of the other. Consequently, the software ultimately chosen is usually a function of the software that is best known to the person recommending it, rather than the needs of the individual.

Choosing a concept map

Unfortunately surveys of concept maps, as with other software, are limited in their usefulness since as soon as somebody highlights a significant difference, the software could be reprogrammed. Furthermore, when screenshots are shown for comparison, they are rarely mapping the same ideas. Therefore comparison is difficult. However, as a starting point, you may like to try: http://en.wikipedia.org/wiki/List_of_Mind_Mapping_software or http://en.wikipedia.org/wiki/List_of_concept_mapping_software. You can also find regular updates and product information at http://mindmappingsoftwareblog.com/.

With online speed becoming faster, 'The Cloud' (online) computing becomes more common. This has led to the new generation of online concept mapping tools, with costs dramatically reduced. There are now many free tools, including some that allow collaborative working. In order to compete with these, the traditional stand-alone version (e.g., Inspiration and the children's version Kidspiration, Mind Manager, Mind Genius and MindFull to name but a few) have had to rethink their strategies. Many are now offering limited online versions for free, with the paid version offering more online storage and greater use of illustrations. As the free versions have an impact (and following) so they too are revising their services and limiting the use unless some sort of annual licence is paid.

Emerging changes to concept mapping

Four significant changes in the past few years have occurred that will help revolutionize at least the use of concept maps if not teaching itself. These are:

1. Integration of sound recording.
2. Use of speech-to-text.
3. Online and collaborative concept maps.
4. Availability in different languages.

The interpretation of sound recording and speech-to-text is a natural progression and will make concept mapping easier as well as create new opportunies for teaching and learning.

Online and collaborative concept maps

Advanced programming techniques, particularly those related to the internet, have led to the rapid rise of online concept maps. These tools operate in real time in a similar manner to the stand-alone versions, with at least one manufacturer already exploring its potential of moving totally to the internet. Not only can software updates be integrated more quickly, but also the libraries can become bigger and shared.

One upside of the online version is the potential to work collaboratively, such as when a tutor assists a dyslexic student even though they are in different geographic locations. However, the downside is that teachers and lecturers are unsure as to whose work they are looking at. The concerns of authorship have always existed, but the internet increases them. It was one thing to have a friend over to help with the homework, as it means somebody has to physically be there, and there could be physical evidence in the form of somebody seeing them. However, with online collaboration, nobody sees who helps, nor their intellectual level. This opens the door to the nasty subject of plagiarism (see Chapter 7).

 Author's Choice: I tell everybody to try concept maps, but have not been a great lover of them myself. That is until I tried ikonmaps. It is so quick, simple and easy to use, and even multilingual (www.ikonmap.com).

Another way in which life is changing is that many teachers are now using concept maps as a way to teach the whole class. Using a whiteboard at the front of the class, everybody can see and contribute to the development of a topic concept map, and the final result can be shared with all the class through the school network.

Research on assistive technology

It is difficult to perform good quality research on assistive technology. There have been some attempts, most of which showed positive results. Lange et al. (2006) assessed four assistive software tools (speech synthesis, spellchecker, homophone tool, and dictionary in Read and Write Gold) as a compensatory strategy for literacy in secondary school, against Microsoft Word. Post-tests showed an improvement for both tested groups in spelling error detection, and word meanings, but worse performance for the Word group in homophone error detection.

Two dimensions versus linear

Concept maps are wonderful tools for mapping out ideas. However, many people forget that in many circumstances the ultimate goal is to create an essay. This is a linear format, with a start, a middle and an end. It is not a two-dimensional visual representation. Somehow a way must be found to move from one format to the other. Most of the concept mapping software has a function in the menus that says 'Export to Word' or similar. This will make it look like a structure for an essay. But how did the software know which was the first or second paragraph? How can it suggest an order when it does not know the priorities? The answer is that it cannot know unless it is told. So having a function that allows re-ordering is of little use unless you know why you are re-ordering and what the best order is. This part is frequently under-emphasized in training and support, yet is one of the most difficult parts for the dyslexic individual. Clear methods need to be explicitly taught for transforming the visual map into a piece that will be acceptable to the recipient. Without it, the essay may still lack structure, and fail to impress examiners who mark using criteria based on a linear format.

Is it an essay?

Some dyslexic individuals have argued that if the concept map is a clear demonstration of knowledge in term of ideas and their relationships, why can they not be submitted for exams? The answer is that it depends on the subject matter. If the purpose of an exam is only to demonstrate knowledge and relationships, then clearly the concept map is all that is required. However, if the exam is intended to show that a person not only knows the relationships, but also can demonstrate their relative importance (a hierarchical structure) and can produce work that conforms to the standards in the field (which is usually an essay, article or research paper), then it is legitimate for the examiner to demand an appropriate format.

The difficulties of marking concept maps (see Chapter 7 and the website for more details) should not be a barrier to submitting concept maps in electronic or other formats. The examination should not measure the disability rather than the ability. However, it should also ensure the results do everything the task intended, and not just part of it.

In conclusion, there is little doubt that getting ideas down on paper, in an acceptable, traditional linear format is one of the biggest problems for the dyslexic individual. Furthermore, many dyslexia support tutors say that this is the greatest area of support that students request at college and university. Concept mapping tools are diverse, with online possibilities creating the potential to radically change software quickly and easily, and to offer alternative formats without problems. The introduction of speech-driven concept mapping has changed the way that you can interact with this software. But, in the end, it is still only a concept map. Unless you can have a fair way to evaluate a concept map, or can turn it into a linear form that really makes sense, you will still need to learn the step of organizing a concept map as an essay.

> ### Mind mapping on the move
>
> With phones such as the iPhone and BlackBerry, not to mention many smart phones, becoming key business tools, it is hardly surprising that mobile versions of concept mapping are becoming popular. Products such as Mindberry and Mindmaker provide insight into how some software may develop in future. Of particular note is how the principle may have to change to the demands of the screen resolution as well as the physical size of the device.

Alternative formats – using timelines

There are times when a traditional concept map may not be appropriate, such as when trying to map out relationships on a time basis, e.g. when planning an essay on World War I. Software such as Timelines (www.timelinemaker.com) is one possible solution, where the 'concept map' becomes linear. Well worth considering in certain instances.

Validation and proofreading

It is no use preparing a long essay if what has been written does not reflect the thoughts of the author. Validation refers to making sure it says what was intended, and this can be broken down into three stages:

1. Spellchecking.
2. Grammar checking.
3. Proofreading.

Spelling and grammar checking

In principle, spellchecking works at the single word level – either the word is spelled right or wrong. However, homophones (e.g., 'there' and 'their', or 'two', 'too' and 'to' or even 'paw', 'poor', 'pour' and 'pore') make it a little more complicated. But the problem for the dyslexic individual if considered at this level is that the word may be spelled correctly, but is the wrong word, i.e. the word exists in the dictionary but is wrong in the particular context, e.g. 'There is two books.' This error can be determined from the context, and requires a grammar checker.

The usefulness of the spellchecker will depend upon the algorithms used, including the extent to which correct spellings occur high up in the list of possible alternatives, the ability to find the right word even when the spelling is far from the target word, and the way in which homophones are handled. That is, the usefulness of the spellchecker will depend upon the ability of the user to easily find the correct word from alternatives offered. Unfortunately, few students are taught how to access and use this tool effectively.

Various spelling and grammar checkers exist, with differing levels of accuracy and quality. Microsoft Word has built-in spelling and grammar checkers. However, the stand-alone specialist software offers far better results. The better software will have the most likely alternative at the top of the list. Otherwise the selection may not be any better than the original.

Proofreading

Text-to-speech software is the ideal tool for dyslexic individuals, since they can concentrate on the comprehension as they listen to the text. Software that highlights which part of the text is being read can make proofreading even easier.

Spelling and grammar checkers – the future

By developing online application, there is the potential to use all the information in the world to compare and contrast with what you have written. At one level this means you can check plagiarism. But at the other end of the scale you can look at spelling and grammar to decide if what you have written is correct in the context. This opens up a whole new world, using the world to check what you have written. One already existing site that uses these principles is Ginger (www.gingersoftware.com).

Predictive software

Predictive software attempts to suggest which word to use next, providing short cuts to make choices. The probabilistic algorithms provide a reasonable level of prediction, but there are doubts about the overall usefulness of this compared with other software such as spelling and grammar checkers. Therefore, this is not considered a priority in the development of software to support the dyslexic student.

Other assistive technology to help dyslexic individuals

When discussing assistive technology with respect to dyslexia, a whole host of software and strategies can help. Most are related directly or indirectly to memory issues. That is, most dyslexic individuals have some issues related to memory over and above those of literacy learning. These can affect many areas from time management to data protection. It may be argued that some of these are about good practice. However, they are related to the use of technology, and frequently there are software solutions. The following highlight the key areas where ICT can help dyslexic individuals with their work and life skills.

Storage and back-up

There are two solutions to back up: hardware and software. The hardware solutions were discussed in Chapter 3. In a quick survey of how often people back-up their data, one-third of the respondents said never, and one-third said 'Once in a blue moon.' Only 10 per cent did it daily. Given the dyslexic individual is not renowned for memory skills, it would seem reasonable to assume that these figures are optimistic for them. Nobody denies how important back-up is, but it is often only when we hear of a colleague's disaster that we remember to back-up. Many of these ideas seem common sense. But when you add the difficulties of the dyslexic individual, even simple tasks such as remembering to remove the USB memory stick from the computer (if the thief is going to take the computer, he or she will take the USB as well so you could lose the back-up too!) can be problematic without effective memory strategies in place. But whatever is chosen, you still have to remember to do the back-up, and to separate the two sets of files.

Examples of back-up services include Dropbox and Carbonite. For a comprehensive and up-to-date comparison of back-up systems, consult www.backupreview.info/.

> ### Recovering deleted files
>
> Do you ever delete a file and then realize you have deleted the wrong one? Fortunately, that file may still be there, even if you emptied the Trash. Software such as Undelete Plus and FreeUndelete are designed to find all undeleted files and help restore them. However, they do have a caveat which is that it depends if they have been overwritten. But data are recoverable in most instances.

Password management options

Password management is about keeping information hidden from others but at the same time having it accessible for when you need it. It also means having access to that information by just remembering one password.

Many dyslexic individuals can use a login for years, but in a time of stress can suddenly no longer be able to recall the password. (It would be wrong to say forget, since they can often recall it later when the stress has gone.) And of course it is not just the password one can forget, there is also the User Name.

There are two password management options – online and offline. Both are easy to use but if you use a number of passwords offline, such as to protect your personal details held in an Excel spreadsheet, you may want to consider an offline version. Probably the most popular offline specialist version is KeePass (www.keepass.com), which has one password to enter a file that can contain every other password. It is free and has been around for many years. Furthermore, you can transfer the file to a USB memory stick so it is with you at all times.

The alternative is to use an online version. Many people are nervous about uploading their passwords to a public place. However, recently developers are offering a solution which encrypts the details locally (i.e. on your computer) before uploading to their website. This means that even if somebody hacked into their site, they still would not be able to access your details. Examples include: Passpack, Clipperz and Boxknox. (NB Boxknox uses pictures as an alternative form of password protection.)

Passwords for Excel spreadsheets

Excel spreadsheets are not the best solution for storing passwords. But if you really do not have an alternative, at least put a password on it. To do this, when you use Save As, there is an option called Tools where you will find General Options. There you will find a place to enter a password. But be sure to have a copy in a safe place (not on the computer!). See also 'ICED number' below.

ICED number

An ICE phone number is the 'In Case of Emergencies' number that is recommended that everybody should hold on their mobile phones. All dyslexic individuals could have their ICED list – In Case of Emergency Dyslexia list. Although originally designed by the East Anglian Ambulance Trust as a help for medical emergencies (the idea is that you put ICE in front of the phone number or name of the person who needs to be contacted in a medical emergency), it could be used as a convention for storing information, such as a 'Note' that contains all the basic information, such as name, phone number, school, doctor, software passwords and any other relevant information. If the phone is lost (e.g., at school), it becomes simple to find out whose it is.

Stickies/Post-its and other desktop reminders

There are many small programs that are available which can sit on the desktop as reminders for urgent tasks, shopping lists or as a simple reminder. These can be with or without some form of alarm. These are excellent for the dyslexic individual who needs some form of visual (and auditory) reminder. The problem is that they can be too convenient, and quickly people can find their desktops are covered in these reminders. Therefore vigilance is required. If used wisely, they can be the perfect memory tool, since it is possible to set colours (for priorities) and alarms for deadlines.

The simplest type is a small stand-alone note that sits on the desktop. There are many examples including Zhorn Stickies and Yahoo Widgets, both of which have built-in alarms. Windows 7 also has built-in stickies.

A second form of 'stickie' is available, which can be regarded as a cross between stickies and concept mapping. This allows you to put down lots of ideas on separate stickies and then re-arrange them. More importantly, they all sit within a single frame since they are made within another program. This means they can be hidden more easily (see, e.g., Microsoft's StickieSorter).

Other types include browser-based reminders such as Sticky Note for iGoogle, online notebooks such as Fruitnotes, and scrapbooks like Knowledge Workshop.

 Author's Choice: Zhorn Stickies are one of the simplest and easiest to use. It lets you have traditional yellow notes on your desktop, with alarms, and all sorts of adaptations. Yet at the same time it can be very simple. Just click on the Task Bar icon, and up pops another yellow note.

Reminders by text or email

Another very useful category is those reminder tools that can send a message as text and email messages. These are very useful especially given the wide availability of smart phones with email capability. (The text messages cost money, so email is better for most people.) Examples include: Remember the milk, Superminder and Mindmeto. Ones more suited to education include: Soshiku, TrackClass, Beat the Deadline, and isdueon.

Time management

Nothing can really make you do things you do not want to do. A computer cannot manage your time, but it can be set to help you. For example, Keepmeout could block you from your favourite social network site if you find yourself visiting it too often. Manictime, AppActivity and TimeSprite can tell you how much time you spent (wasted?) on each activity.

 Author's Choice: Marxio Timer is a timer/stopwatch, but it does other things too. Not only can it be used as a simple countdown timer, but it also turns off the computer, runs specific programs, clicks set points at a set time, etc. So, e.g., it could be set to double click on a desktop icon at a specific time.

Research

These are a number of tools that may help with online research, whether it is for academic reasons, work or pleasure. Many dyslexics have problems with research, and in particular internet-based research.

Fortunately there are several types of tools now available to help track where you are, where you have been and what notes you took. This can help remember details (including avoiding accidental plagiarism) and provide assistance in structuring the work. Examples include Zotero, Yahoo Search Pad and related tools such as Mendeley.

Sound recording software

There are many uses of sound recording software, and many commercial and free software packages for sound recording, (see, e.g., Audacity – http://audacity.sourceforge.net). Sound recording hardware was discussed in Chapter 3 and here we shall simply talk about the software. This can be used for recording, playback and editing. As with the hardware, the quality will depend on the quality of the microphone, and the ambient sound. However, with computers it is also useful to check the noise made by the mains power connection. (Simply compare the sound levels when the mains is unplugged with when it is plugged in.)

As well as standard recording software, there are also specialist applications, such as Pamela for Skype (www.pamela-software.com) and Callburner which can record Skype conversations.

Screen recording

For those who may want to record the screen (e.g., to show somebody how to use software or to remember how something was done), there are a number of free software programs, including Jing, Camstudio and Screentoaster.

Recording and note taking

OneNote from Microsoft and Lecturer Recorder combine sound recording and note taking in a single piece of software. With this (and several similar pieces of software), it is possible to synchronize the audio of a lecture (e.g., using a good directional microphone) and the notes you type at the same time. Clearly this saves a lot of time trying to match notes to the right part of the recording.

On-screen magnifiers

Many dyslexic individuals prefer to view text on-screen at a slightly higher magnification than others. This could be adjusted by changing the screen resolution, using zoom in a given software, or use some form of on-screen magnifier. Examples include Microsoft's Zoom It, Iconico's Magnifier and those inside other software, such as PicPick (many more can be found at www.magnifiers.org). Traditionally these simply magnify the whole screen or part of it. However, some will grey out the areas outside the main interest area to offer a more focused approach. One example is Claro's Lightening Magnifier.

Screensharing and video conferencing

Although more fully discussed in Chapter 7, it is worth making a quick mention of a group of software systems that allow remote support and collaboration. Examples include Dimdim, Mikogo and Elluminate.

Data sharing

An increasing number of online document (or working environment) sharing websites allow two or more people to work on a document at the same time. This is different from screensharing since it centres on the specific shared document, rather than being a shared environment. Examples include:

- Spreadsheets – Editgrid
- Word processing – Shutterborg, Etherpad
- Drawing and whiteboards – Scribblar, Scriblink
- Office – Google Docs, ShowDocument.

Training in using assistive technology

Too many individuals who buy or are given assistive technology fail to engage with its potential. The most common reason for this is that they have been provided with the technology but without the necessary training. Thus, much of the money spent is wasted.

Where training is provided, it is often at the very beginning of the use of the software, where you can only take in so much. Once the basics have been learned, then there needs to be further training to show what else could be achieved. This is true of everybody, but particularly true of the dyslexic individual, where memory and information overload are often a problem.

Teachers and support tutors as well as technical support in businesses rarely have the time available to provide all the necessary assistance and are not always familiar with the technology. The alternative therefore is to develop self-support systems which provide maximum empowerment with additional support where necessary.

Several EU projects have recognized that logistically and economically it would be difficult to provide the numbers of trained assistive technology support personnel required to support dyslexic students at university. Basic guides to using technology were developed in Dystrain, iSheds, Embed and Dessdys, details of which are to be found on the accompanying website.

Fortunately a number of manufacturers are now providing basic video guides for their software, and on-screen demonstrations of how to get the most from it. As well as the EU projects, there are several sources for generic information, such as the CD-based Aspire Active Learning Videos from Claro Software. These will continue to expand in the coming years.

Finally, while there is little doubt that support in a YouTube culture will be dominated by self-learning videos, it is important to remember that blended learning, mixing the technology-based learning with human support, is key not only for the dyslexic individual but for most learners.

Conclusion

Ultimately, unless you match the technology to the specific needs of the individual, the software may prove to be useless. You could liken it to a prescription for glasses – unless the prescription is just right, benefits are limited. However, the precision of the optometrist in deciding what is required is far greater than in specifying assistive technology, not least because the 'feedback' is so conspicuous. Also, unlike the reading glasses that are suitable for reading at that one distance no matter what the material, the particular software may need to be different depending on the circumstances.

Most of the decisions made when choosing software are based on overall needs and relating them to software categories (e.g., text-to-speech) rather than going into details about the pros and cons of each software package. Part of that is because the differences are small, and if you specify one piece of software based on that difference, the other software may change to the same specification. The rapidity of change in the technology makes it difficult for dyslexic assessors to keep abreast of all the changes and new developments. While continuing professional development courses can help keep people up to date, there is a lack of suitable mechanisms to ensure that dyslexic people receive the most appropriate choice at the time of their assessment.

There is little doubt that ten years ago the provision of technology for dyslexic individuals made a huge difference. What is missing is a real understanding of the technology, both in terms of its potential and its availability. There is a huge potential to support all dyslexic individuals through assistive technology by a paradigm shift. But only when representatives of the users, technologists and funders come together, will there be a change that allows every dyslexic individual to use the technology to help them reach their potential.

5

Literacy Learning Software

Introduction

This chapter is about literacy learning software – that is, software that you will use, learn from, and then discard after having acquired those skills. Given the nature of dyslexia, where over-learning is the rule rather than the exception, it will often be necessary to return again and again to the software, but eventually it will not be needed.

Many educationalists say that the primary years are about learning to read, while the secondary school years are about reading to learn. Unless you have mastered the fundamental skills of decoding the printed word, you will not be able to use that skill to extract information from books. But 'reading' is really a euphemism for a much wider collection of skills, including reading comprehension, spelling and writing at length. Furthermore, those literacy skills require a combination of what may be considered intrinsic skills (such as short-term memory) and underlying literacy skills (such as phonological analysis skills).

From a developmental perspective, most children reach a maturity whereby they have the underlying cognitive skills to have the potential to learn the cognitive literacy skills such as rhyming, alliteration, syllable counting, etc. This happens in tandem with literacy acquisition, where reading improves phonological skills, and improved phonological skills lead to improvements in literacy skills.

Morais et al. (1987) demonstrated that adult illiterate individuals have not acquired phonological skills, highlighting that they are acquired, rather than developmental, skills. Traditionally we talk about improving memory skills, knowing that what we are really doing is finding strategies to overcome the difficulties, rather than improving the actual skills. But if we can improve other fundamental skills, then maybe we can also improve the memory itself. The problem is not about finding ways to improve memory, but in showing that those skills have improved beyond the training methods, and that they are lasting.

Conversely, it could be suggested that it is irrelevant if the memory itself has improved, or strategies have been found, as long as the main skill (e.g., reading) has been improved. In the short term, that may be true. But in the long term, if you do not improve the fundamental skills, you will have to find a strategy for every process.

How can computers help? The advantage the computer offers in all this is the potential to allow repetition (structured and sequential) and to monitor the impact. Changes will not happen overnight. Indeed, it may take many months of practice to see a change. This is why it is important to understand the principles of the software, what is claimed and if it works. Without that knowledge, months of valuable learning time could be wasted. However, the problem is that the software is only as good as the research behind it, and even that at times is dubious.

In this chapter we shall review some of the key issues that educationalists have to face when choosing appropriate literacy learning software.

The teaching, learning and testing cycle

The assessment process is normally seen as a discrete process that can indicate what an individual can and cannot do. It provides a baseline to the learning process against which any teaching can be measured. Clearly, if over the course of time the teaching input has not made a significant impact upon the level acquired, as measured by the assessment process, then the learning is limited (or the testing process is significantly flawed). When it comes to learning software, the assessment process is often implicit, in that, in order to progress, the software must measure if there has been some learning. In the same way a computer game will see if you have 'collected enough treasure to advance to the next level', so too the literacy software (often game-based) will also measure the treasure (skills) collected before moving up to the next level. However, the measure is with respect to the specific activity, and not necessarily to an underlying skill. The question is, what underlying skill(s) does the activity address?

In order to address this issue, let us consider four key areas:

1. *The software is testing, not teaching.* Unfortunately too much software is only looking for right answers, without evaluating why the answer was wrong and providing feedback/learning. By using adaptive testing in the learning environment, the software can be made to channel the user to the most appropriate next section. Put simply, if the computer asks 'What is 3 x 4?' and the child answers '7', clearly he or she has added and not multiplied. If this was a consistent error, then the system needs to return to the fundamentals of multiplication. Without this explicit understanding of learning, progress would, at best, be limited. Many non-dyslexic children will pick up the principles implicitly. But the dyslexic individual has greater difficulty with the task and therefore, if this is aimed at the dyslexic individual, it will fail the very group it is intended to support.

2. *Computer software has its limitations.* If the work was being carried out with a tutor, the child could be encouraged to guess, explore, analyse and manipulate the sounds, and build up an idea of how to solve the problem. The tutor would be constantly measuring the responses, and providing feedback based on those responses. Unfortunately the computer is still not good enough to provide such high levels of context-dependent feedback as is required in the learning process, particularly where the child is failing to learn. Even with the most sophisticated software, there is usually an assumption that a teacher is close at hand to offer additional support. That does not mean that technically it cannot be achieved. There is already a number of language learning software packages available which allow you to speak a word or phrase, and the software evaluates your pronunciation against the target sound. This is not so different from the idea of sounding out syllables or identifying rhymes. However, this is the type of activity one can expect in the future.

3. *Computer programmers have their limitations.* Although things are changing rapidly, the traditional approach to development of software for the dyslexic individual has been to move from a well-intentioned concept to the final product without involving the 'wider user group' which includes dyslexic individuals with diverse strengths and weaknesses, as well as those supporting them. This is usually due to the financial constraints, both for development and the amount people will pay for software.

4. *Does the software teach what is claimed?* Let us say that the child uses a game for two months, and improves from random guessing to correct 95 per cent of the time. Can we say the child has learned and, if so, what has he or she learned? Clearly he or she will have learned to do better at the game. But is that because he or she has learned a strategy that is specific to the game or learned the skill? (Is it random every time, or has the child remembered the sequence? Are the alternatives limited? Is there something else within the test items that could suggest the correct answer and not just the intended skills?) And, more importantly, what is the impact on his or her literacy skills? The only 'measure' is that he or she has moved to the next level. Unfortunately it is not always clear whether the child has acquired the skill and that skill will be retained, or if he or she has simply learned strategies to solve the task, collect the 'treasure' and go to the next level.

The way to test is to use an independent measure, delivered by an independent person without access to the learning (to avoid bias). The problem with this theoretical scenario is that of 'independence'. What do you use to measure? And who is going to pay somebody to be totally independent? Furthermore, researchers do not as a rule wish to prove that somebody else's commercial work is worth buying.

Finally, there is the long-term impact of the activity. Occasionally an 'independent' student may carry out unpaid research as part of his or her studies. However, this is by its very nature a short-term activity, with little opportunity to learn, and rarely a chance to ensure the retention of the information over a reasonable time period. Furthermore, his or her limited experience often means that it is not as in-depth as required.

The issues above highlight some of the problems faced by developers, researchers, funders and evaluators, and it against this background that we can look for ways to overcome the problems.

Cognitive skills software

In Chapter 1, a model was presented which highlighted the underlying cognitive skills that underpin reading and writing, at least at the single word level. Research suggests that each 'module' can be considered an independent component, and that as such it would therefore be possible to teach the skills of these domains in various combinations (since it is almost impossible to improve just one skill).

Memory

There are three memories in principle that we need to consider: (1) auditory memory; (2) visual memory; and (3) working memory. These are often described in different ways but, for the purpose of this discussion, the main distinction is that auditory memory and visual memory refer to the short-term storage and retrieval of information without any intervening manipulation of that information. For working memory, there is an explicit manipulation of the data, whatever that may be. Although there is much work on the general population (see, e.g., the work of Alloway et al. 2004, 2006, etc.), there is very little published independent peer review research with respect to memory training software and the dyslexic individual.

Two unpublished theses (Szpala 1997; Aspinall 1999), reported on a memory software developers' website, suggested an improved memory after only a small amount of training. In a small intervention (only four sessions over a four-week period), Szpala (1997) reported 'significant' improvement in three of seven tests on the British Ability Scales seen as a consequence of improved working memory. (effects were seen on Recall of Objects Verbal Immediate, Recall of Objects Spatial Immediate, Recall of Digits Backwards, but no significant results were found on: Recall of Digits Forward, Recall of Designs, Recall of Objects Verbal Delayed, Recall of Objects Spatial Delayed). This suggests that there is an impact beyond the training, but that may be specific to areas of training. Furthermore, it was also found that where there were effects, those who had additional instruction made better progress than those without instruction. This transfer of skills for that software was confirmed by Aspinall (1999) who, after six sessions of training over three weeks, found effects for both visual-only training and visual/auditory strategies.

There has also been work in related fields such as that of ADHD, where advances in apparent memory skills in one task have carried over to another area (see, e.g., Klingberg et al. 2002, 2005). Furthermore, these studies reported improvements in response inhibition, attention and reasoning.

In 2008, McPherson and Burns looked at the validity of using computer game-like tests which point to one future direction. Although there is little in the way of games to improve these skills, it does suggest a way forward. That said, the EU project Edysgate (see p. 105) provides an insight into what may be possible. The project did not attempt to prove its ability to improve the specific skills, but this research tends to suggest that activities like this are worthy of further consideration.

Literacy development software

Literacy development is about practising the skills that allow one to extract information from the page (decoding) and understand what the writer is trying to say, plus write one's own thoughts in a way that others will understand (encoding), and to perform these skills accurately and fluently.

The computer offers the potential to teach these skills by providing the structured, sequential, multi-sensory teaching necessary for the dyslexic individual. It has many advantages over 'human intervention' such as less specialist knowledge required, and the motivational aspects of the computer. In this, the apparent non-judgemental aspect should not be underestimated. However, the skills go beyond those listed in the research section.

Consideration should also be given to the manner of teaching. No one skill is taught in isolation. Furthermore, typing skills can have a significant impact on the speed and enjoyment of the activities (see Chapter 4). For this reason, many, though not all, of the computer-based activities teach typing skills at the same time as phonics, using the motor memory to reinforce the letter sequences. These are generally based either on the Hornsby Alpha to Omega system (Hornsby and Shear 1975) or the Orton-Gillingham principles. However, a number of activities have been developed by researchers based on their published research, or by independent persons/groups. In all cases it is recommended to confirm the background of the intervention. This is particularly so for those programs which were originally developed for other learning groups (e.g., a program developed for adults but adapted for use with children) or presented in a language that is different from that of the original research.

Case study 4 Edysgate

The aim of this EU (Grundtvig)-funded project was to provide exercises not on literacy, but on the underlying cognitive skills that help support reading and writing. Such games and activities are widely available for children either as explicit teaching, or implicit learning through diverse computer-based games. However, few are aimed at the older person. Young dyslexic adults do not like them due to their childish nature or because they seem irrelevant.

This project aimed to provide a highly motivating and stimulating learning environment for a carefully selected range of skills known to be important for young dyslexic adults. It addressed seven areas of particular importance for vocational skills development. The areas were targeted through direct and indirect stimulation.

The principles behind the exercises are not specific to any given language – they will work for all individuals across Europe. The exercises are developed in collaboration with the user groups as well as those who train them.

The work concentrates on the principal domains of:

- auditory discrimination
- auditory memory
- auditory sequential memory
- visual discrimination
- visual memory
- visual sequential memory
- visual spatial memory.

The diverse activities are constructed in Flash, and can be played through any internet connected computer. The results are stored for later analysis. There was no quantitative analysis of the effectiveness of the activities. However, they did provide a suite of games (135 games altogether) that would enable further researchers to carry out more detailed studies. The project won a global UNESCO award in 2008 and a following project, Dys2 (www.dys2.org) started in November 2009.

Literacy-related software research

There are many potential sources of research reviews for 'paper-based' intervention (see, e.g., Snowling 2000; Reid 2003: Singleton 2009). The aim of this section is to provide a brief overview of research that demonstrates the potential to use the computer as a tool to support the dyslexic individual. The following studies represent some of the more significant contributions to the field. The following research represents some of the most significant contributions in the field, however, they should be treated with respect regarding the criteria discussed in the section on peer review (p. 111).

Unfortunately there is a shortage of good research that specifically looks at how the technology can support the dyslexic individual. That which does, e.g., Ecalle et al. (2009); Tijms and Hoeks (2005); Irausquin et al. (2005), shows good positive results. As a consequence of this shortage, one therefore has to report results which demonstrate the advantages in the general population and suggest that these results may be generalizable to the dyslexic individual. The research cited here highlights some of the more significant results. For wider reviews, one should consult papers, e.g., Blok et al. (2002); Knezek and Christensen (2008). However, this again highlights the problem that any review will itself be looking at old research, and with the delays in publication, it is not easy to find research that takes full advantage of recent advances in technology and of programming techniques.

Using multimedia

In seeking to identify the important parts of multimedia learning and the relative effects of the different components, a number of researchers have noted that it is not simply a matter of ensuring there is text, sound and pictures. A number of researchers (Alty and Beacham 2006: Mayer and Moreno 1998; Morano and Mayer 1999a, 1999b) have developed a theoretical construct to demonstrate how integration of multimedia can assist all learners, which is relevant to the dyslexic learner (Alty and Beacham, 2006). They state that the multiple representation principle suggests using words and pictures is better than words alone, that the contiguity principle suggests the words should match the pictures, and the coherence principle is that the less extraneous words and sounds, the better it is. Furthermore, they suggest that it is better to present auditory and narration without the corresponding on-screen text. This appears to be in line with the principles of multi-sensory learning with dyslexic students. However, some (e.g., Gyarmathy 2006) would suggest that in some cases implicit learning is beneficial to the dyslexic learner, citing the case of on-screen single words to reinforce learning in a language learning context for dyslexic individuals.

Whiting and Chapman (2000) also found that using visual, auditory and kinaesthetic input for a computer-based typing, reading and spelling program, plus positive reinforcement, provided benefits to those who were previously failing in literacy acquisition.

Underwood (2000) looked at the claims made about using multimedia with development of reading skills, comparing results between structured sub-skills tutoring (using Integrated Learning System – drill and practice software, namely SuccessMaker) versus free reading using a talking book. Results suggest that learning does occur but not necessarily as expected. Furthermore, it was suggested that the characteristics of the software and motivation can be more important than any discussion on the level of phonics involved.

Several studies have used Fast ForWord® (FFW) as an intervention method, with mixed results. The US government-sponsored web institute of Educational Science reports that five studies of Fast ForWord® met their evidence standards and one study met What Works Clearinghouse (WWC) evidence standards with reservations. They concluded that the program had 'positive effects on alphabetics and mixed effects on comprehension'. They also noted that 'No studies that met WWC evidence standards with or without reservations addressed fluency or general reading achievement'; see http://ies.ed.gov/ncee/wwc/pdf/WWC_Fast_Forword_070907.pdf. Research includes that by Hook et al. (2001) who reported trials, comparing computer-based intervention results with those using traditional Orton-Gillingham (OG) methods. Both groups improved in phonemic awareness, but only OG showed gains in the ability to decode, pronounce and understand words, and these were maintained over two years. Other research (Agnew et al. 2004) found the program improved auditory temporal discrimination but that this did not generalize to reading-related skills, namely phonological awareness and non-word reading.

It is difficult to differentiate between the motivational, novelty and neutral nature of computer-based learning, as opposed to the pure pedagogical advantage of the systems. The lack of quality research and the difficulty of replication and independence make comparisons difficult (Soe et al. 2000). That said, given enough time, and a commitment to pursue evidence-based systems that are evaluated independently, there is little doubt that the computer-based reading program can offer much to the dyslexic individual since the level can be tailored to needs.

Phonics

Dyslexia-specific work on phonics includes that of Ecalle et al. (2009), Tijms and Hoeks (2005) and Irausquin et al. (2005). In the research by Ecalle et al. (2009), in French, they taught underlying phonological skills and found improvements in both reading and spelling. In Dutch, Tijms and Hoeks (2005) focused on the recognition and use of phonological and morphological structures. Reading accuracy, reading rate and spelling all improved.

Working with poor readers, Irausquin, Drent and Verhoeven (2005) found that computer-presented speed training led to improved word and text reading efficiency, but did not affect comprehension. Furthermore, the impact appeared to be beyond the simple word structures used in the exercises.

Jiménez et al. (2007) studied four types of computer-based reading training procedures (in Spanish), involving five test groups of children aged between seven and ten: whole word, syllable, onset-rime, phoneme and untrained. The aim was to examine the effects of different spelling-to-sound units in computer speech-based reading. The phoneme and syllable training improved their word recognition in comparison with the control group.

Looking at gains made in computer-assisted remedial reading, Wise et al. (2000) compared 200 students aged seven to 11 who spent 29 hours using two paradigms. The children in the 'accurate-reading-in-context' group spent 22 individualized computer hours reading stories plus seven hours learning comprehension strategies in small groups. These children's reading gained more in time-limited word reading than the group who had 'phonological-analysis' training for seven hours, with the time on the computer being divided between phonological exercises and story reading. However, this 'phonological' group gained more in phonological skills and untimed word reading. Furthermore, lower-level readers gained more, and benefited more from phonological training, than higher-level readers. Follow-up studies showed that most children maintained or improved their levels and that both groups scored equally on word reading, but the phonologically trained children scored higher on phonological decoding.

Working in the highly regular Finnish language, Hintikka et al. (2005) found that with first graders with poor pre-reading skills, a six-week intervention program with 170 minutes of instruction led to accelerated learning of letter naming, but no significant difference in reading acquisition. However, further analysis showed that the intervention was most effective for those with low phoneme awareness skills and attention difficulties, as noted by the teachers. This highlights the need to look at the impact at the individual level, and not just to review group results.

Furthermore, Lyytinen et al. (2007) suggested that non-dyslexic individuals could improve their basic reading skills (in the transparent

Finnish language) in as little as four hours using their computer software. While they acknowledge for the dyslexic learner it would take a little longer, these techniques could help minimize the difficulties later on.

Other research (Macaruso et al. 2006; Mitchell and Fox 2001; Knezek and Christensen 2008) also suggests that first graders develop good phonics skills using computer-based programs.

Teachers' perceptions of Wordshark

A research report by Singleton and Simmons (2000) reflected on the classroom use of Wordshark, an edutainment (education using entertainment) package designed to improve child's spelling and word recognition skills. The content is based on the widely used Alpha to Omega synthetic phonics system (Hornsby and Shear 1975). Using questionnaires, the researchers found the 86.6 per cent of schools used the software frequently with SEN children, and 54.6 per cent used software with non-SEN kids at some point. The software was employed in many ways, with 94 per cent reporting using it to practise words, 63 per cent for new words, and 95 per cent for reinforcing teaching points such as consonant blends. The motivational aspect is reflected as 49 per cent used it as some form of reward. Teachers' rating suggest the children, and particularly dyslexic children, were considerably more motivated to use the program compared to participating in similar classroom activities. Some 60 per cent suggested that there was some improvement in reading and spelling skills, with about one quarter registering a 'substantial' improvement.

However, as with much of the research in this field, the results need to be treated with caution since there is no comparison. That is, this is not about comparing the impact of one computer-based software against another to provide clear evidence of relative efficacy, but about the apparent perceptions of teachers, and the motivational impact of using computer-based learning.

Phonics and typing skills

Touch-Type Read and Spell (TTRS) uses the principles of Hornsby and Shear's Alpha to Omega to provide keyboard skills program. Stephens (2000) found significant gains in the reading and spelling ages after four months of training. Furthermore, questionnaires suggested that the learners felt that the program had also improved their academic self-confidence and motivation.

Comprehension

Elkind (1998) trained students to use a computer-assisted reading program (Kurzweil 3000) and were tested and retested using the Nelson Denny Reading Test of comprehension. Improvements in reading rates, comprehension, and the benefits of utilizing an auditory and visual integrative approach for reading were found. These findings were also found in similar studies conducted on students with significant reading disabilities and attention disorders (Hecker et al. 2002). Elkind also suggested that not only do they increase comprehension (through the ability to concentrate on meaning rather than decoding at the single word level) but also they can sustain the 'reading' for longer.

Using speech recognition software, Raskind and Higgins (1999) studied a group of 39 students in elementary and secondary school. Results indicated improvements in phonological processing as identified in improved word recognition, spelling, and reading comprehension.

Using speech-to-text

Although there is plenty of anecdotal evidence to suggest that speech-to-text helps dyslexic students, there is a lack of research with dyslexic individuals to back this up. However, results from the Project Listen Reading Tutor program with Grades 1–4 (Mostow et al. 2002) suggested that using the computer improved word identification, word comprehension, passage comprehension, fluency, phonemic awareness, rapid letter naming, and spelling. This effect was greatest in Grade 1.

In an attempt to overcome the lack of a reliable way to directly measure reading fluency using the computer, Beck et al. (2004) used inter-word latency as an indicator, which produced a correlation (0.78) which increased to 0.83 when one allowed for the help that was asked. Refinement of this method could provide a ready measure of reading fluency evaluation.

As well as being useful for writing, speech-to-text can be used directly for reading. Higgins and Raskind (2000) used both discrete (single word) and continuous speed recognition systems to compare the outcomes with dyslexic users. Discrete (single word) and continuous speech groups showed significant improvements in word recognition and reading comprehension. On cognitive measures, only phonological processing in the discrete speech group showed significant change. However, some of the users did find it very stressful, highlighting the role of personal preferences and difference between dyslexic learners.

Other research

Lomicka (1998) looked at the use of annotations (glossing) of the text for learners of French, and demonstrated that there was an increase in the number of causal inferences generated when the full annotations were available. Although no study has taken place with dyslexic individuals, it would seem logical to assume that this 'glossing' technique would have an even greater benefit for them.

Cobb (2007) demonstrated the use of technology to 'construct' reading programs to help English as an Additional Language students. He presented clear data to demonstrate how it would be possible to ensure the minimum number of occurrences of new words. This technique could also be applied to the development of textbooks for dyslexic readers.

Verezub et al. (2008) found that explicit teaching of metacognitive strategies enhanced comprehension in the hypertext context.

Peer review and review bias

A number of researchers and commentators (e.g., Ashton et al. 2001) have commented on the bias of research related to technology, since it is often carried out by those with a vested interested in the results. Furthermore, reports such as those coming from, e.g., the Software and Information Industry Association may be biased as the authors are not independent education evaluators but are from the software industry itself. This, they suggest, is why only positive outcomes are reported.

Wherever possible, reference in this text has been made to peer reviews of the software. However, due to the nature of the business, it is not always possible to obtain independent evaluations. That is, if a person/corporation develops software, they will want to demonstrate its effectiveness, and may pay somebody to do that research. This undermines the independence of the reviewer. Conversely, who would want to prove somebody else's commercial product is effective if they themselves make no gain as a consequence? This is not to undermine the integrity of the research reported, but to highlight the potential conflicts of interest that can happen, and anybody seeking research that reports efficacy should attempt to consult independent reviews.

One of the most informative sites is the US-based Institute of Education Sciences, which is part of the US Department of Education. For example, it has a section on Beginning Reading (http://ies.ed.gov/ncee/wwc/Reports/

Topic.aspx?tid=01) where reports on the efficacy of various paper- and computer-based programs can be found. Furthermore, they carefully document the criteria used and, importantly, do not restrict themselves to an overview, but, where appropriate, provide information on which parts may be of benefit. However, reports on software widely available to assist the dyslexic individual are limited.

Other areas for literacy development

As well as the basic phonics, there are a number of other areas that are important to learn for the development of fluent and accurate literacy skills. These include grammar, syntax and punctuation, as well as the skills of writing at length.

Grammar, syntax and punctuation of writing

Punctuation is an important aspect, and an area where many dyslexic individuals have problems. It is not uncommon to come across writing that has no punctuation, making it difficult for the reader to comprehend. There are a number of rules that can be learned by the dyslexic individual, using a hierarchical structure of the most important ones first. Using appropriate software to learn is far better than trying to rely on Microsoft Word to guess what was intended!

Writing frames

Although a writing frame may be seen as 'assistive', in most cases they are discarded after a few years since the principles have been learned and can be applied without the specific use. There are various levels of writing frames but, like much of this software, there is little research to support claims to efficiency. But most teachers would agree that their advantages are self-evident. Various types have been introduced over the years. However, there is a growing tendency to make them overly complex. Sometimes something as simple as a PowerPoint template is enough.

Conclusion

There is no doubt that we are just beginning to scratch the surface with literacy learning using computers, despite having had some 20 years of research. The reason we have at one and the same time progressed so far yet achieved little lies in several areas. These include:

- A piece of research from concept to publication may take two years. Consider how much the technology itself can change in that time. So, e.g., the potential has grown in the past year to drastically overhaul the way the material is delivered by using more online monitoring, updating the material available, and providing more suitable content.
- A lot of the research is carried out by students using a single approach in a given area (such as teaching syllabification skills). They do not have the funding to develop it for the market.
- There are few systems that integrate all aspects. Where they do exist, the independent research does not always support the results reported by the developers.
- Where evidence is provided, it is rarely independent. Unless there is independent evidence, who will believe the research?
- There is little dyslexia-related research over and above small programs that only address a few areas.

In theory, we have the methods, not just with multisensory learning objects, but also the Baysian models of learning which permit us to integrate the learning and testing in one seamless package, and deliver customized learning to every child irrespective of their difficulties. The problems, however, are in the development cost of producing such a package, and the need for independent results that show clear advantages of one method over another. Given the positive results that computer-based learning can offer, and the cost-effectiveness of widespread uptake, it is surprising that no government, or inter-governmental agency (such as UNESCO or the World Bank) has attempted to fund an open source system which could provide education for all, allowing adaptations and improvement to suit local needs. One has to ask why this is so.

6

The User Interface

Introduction

Anecdotal evidence over the years suggests that while everybody has their own preferences as to the look and feel of the computer learning and working environment (i.e. the user interface), there are some general guidelines that may help dyslexic individuals. This chapter attempts to bring together the evidence with respect to dyslexic and non-dyslexic individuals (little research is aimed specifically at the dyslexic individual) to provide guidance for those who are making choices. These include those printing paper-based books as well as developers of e-learning and websites.

The evidence is derived from research, projects, reports and recommendations, while also explaining the diverse aspects that need to be considered when considering the dyslexic user.

If we have the opportunity to individualize something, we tend to examine how we can adapt it to our needs. It does not matter if we are talking about the availability of DIY products to modify our homes, or the move to electronic formats (and low-cost colour printers) which relieved us from the pre-set formats of the printed medium. As we are given more freedom to adapt, so we can adjust the specifications to our needs. Adopt, adapt, improve, as someone clever once said.

These adjustments can be made by three distinct parties:

- the architecture specifiers
- the developer of the resources and their legislators
- the end user.

The architecture specifiers are those charged with creating the overall ability for change to be possible, such as specifiers for the latest version of internet code (e.g., HTML 5, which is the next version of internet language which will probably be implemented in browsers even before it is finalized). The Web Accessibility Initiative is also a key player, although its influence has tended to be more with respect to the needs of those with impairment of hearing and vision. This field also includes the developers of the programs used to make electronic format material, such as Adobe (manufacturers of DreamWeaver and Flash). These organizations have a responsibility to listen to the needs of the diverse user groups and to ensure that what they apply does not restrict other user groups.

The developers of resources include web and e-book designers who use software to create their resources. If the tools they use have the capacity to make the content dyslexia-friendly, then they should ensure the appropriate functionality is available. Furthermore, there are official bodies that offer guidelines for others to follow, such as the European Union.

Finally, there is the end user, who often does not know the potential to make changes or how to do it.

All of the above leave a lot to be desired in terms of the information being widely available. It is no good having the necessary functionality if nobody knows it is there.

It is clear that the issues regarding personal preference with respect to the dyslexic individual are not just about people adjusting their own settings. It is a consideration for all those involved in the process. It does not matter if we are talking about a website, formal e-learning, or a CD-based encyclopaedia – all should have the capability to adapt to the needs of the individual, within reason.

Making 'reasonable accommodations' is the way the legislation covers the gap between the demands of user groups and the financial impact of those demands. That is, the user group may want a human voice for an e-book, but funding restrictions make that impractical. A reasonable compromise would be to ensure the text was accessible to text-to-speech. (Note that the case study with respect to Amazon's Kindle mentioned later may make institutions reluctant to implement approaches that could benefit many dyslexic individuals.)

The four main issues

In order to analyse the diverse areas of interest, we need to identify the parameters that could be changed if we had the chance. Traditional discussions of accessibility are with reference to the visually impaired being able to access content with a text reader. In order to provide an appropriate framework for discussion with respect to the dyslexic user, the following categories will be used:

1. Technological issues
2. Navigational issues
3. Typographic issues
4. Layout issues.

Each of these will be discussed in turn. Note, however, that while this is written with particular reference to e-learning, it can also equally apply to the printed word.

Technological issues

Many dyslexic users will use text-to-speech software (see Chapter 4) to listen to e-content. Therefore, to ensure the content can be read by the text-to-speech software, the resource, whether it is a web page, an e-book or other resource, needs to be constructed in a manner that makes it available to text-to-speech (unless there is an audio file to accompany the text). However, some of the text may be in formats that require extra attention to ensure they are accessible to text-to-speech. For example, text that is embedded in Flash animation, or inside a picture, needs to have tags that can be read by the software.

As with all software development it is important to extensively test the material in different environments and in particular with different assistive technology, as they all have their own idiosyncrasies that may impact upon the learning experience for the dyslexic individual. For example, many text-to-speech readers only follow general rules, and cannot always recognize a header (or sometimes bullet points) for what they are. Without a full stop, the software does not register the need for a pause. In order to overcome this, some designers add a full stop at the end of headers and bullet points. This can look ugly in the design but can be hidden by making it very small or the same colour as the background (if the background colour does not change!).

Due consideration should be made as to how the user preferences affect the screen navigation. For example, many dyslexic users prefer a larger font size than that provided by designers. Consequently, the text is frequently seen flowing off screen to the right when using fixed text box sizes. It is also important to ensure that all dialogue boxes (e.g., a Help Menu) and other pop-up text boxes also use the user's preferences.

The principle should be to keep the interface clear and clean, using intuitive navigation at all times. And the only way to ensure this is to invite user feedback, from diverse technological settings. Failure to do so will soon cause frustration and be a disincentive to the acquisition of new knowledge. It has so much to offer and if the simple rules of accessibility and usability are not followed, then the dyslexic users will quickly give up.

Navigational issues

Screen layout is an important and frequently overlooked component for the dyslexic individual. A cursory glance at a dyslexic checklist will highlight the issues, such as easy to confuse, and having problems with remembering instructions. That is why the best learning environments have simple navigation, and a hierarchy that is set to minimize what is on view at any one time. For example, the principal learning environment for the dyslexia-friendly EU project Dystrain had just four buttons – forward, back, play sound and back up one level.

For the dyslexic (and other) users, clarity and simplicity should be more important than 'designer' looks which win awards judged by non-dyslexic individuals. The layout of the page and navigation between pages, sections and functions should be intuitive and consistent. There should be familiarity and cohesion between the diverse parts, providing the knowledge that once you have mastered the environment in the first section, you will never have to master a new environment to finish that course. Even the knowledge that the environment is dyslexic-friendly and can be customized to the users' needs in itself helps relieve stress. However, the customization still has to be done, and some environments make this easier than others.

Ten tips for designers and authors

1. Keep backgrounds clean and eliminate distracting items if they do not add to the learning.
2. Make navigation simple, consistent, easy to learn, use and remember.
3. Make the interface adaptable in colours (background and font) and fonts (type and size).
4. Ensure all components can be accessed by text-to-speech and other assistive technology.
5. For shared learning environments (e.g., chat areas and discussion forums), ensure dyslexia is not a restriction to participation.
6. Keep text width to less than 80 characters, sentences less than 20 words, use bullet points wherever appropriate and left justified.
7. Use methods, systems and conventions that are known to work with dyslexic individuals.
8. In exams ensure that the disability is supported, but the ability is assessed.
9. Run trials with user groups.
10. Provide human support, both as a tutoring method and for technical support.

Typographic issues

Discussing the typographic issues, a range of parameters can be considered. Some may more strictly be considered design and layout issues, but are included here as they form a natural extension of these considerations.

The principal considerations are:

- typeface
- font size
- kerning and ligature
- leading (line spacing)
- justification.

Although already stated previously, in the following it should be remembered that much of the existing research (unless indicated specifically) is with respect to the average reader and not the dyslexic reader. It would not be reasonable to assume the dyslexic user's needs are the same. That said, it is also important to note that any recommendations made by such organizations (e.g., the BDA) are based on the personal opinions of a small number of people and their own experience. While these may be representative of a wider community, there is little evidence to confirm this. In a day and age when decisions need to be evidence-based, the following is written to provide insight into the decision-making process, and hopefully inspire others to develop research that will inform these decisions, particularly with respect to dyslexic individuals.

Typefaces

A great deal of rhetoric has been written over the years about which is the best typeface to use for dyslexic individuals. It would be easy to cite references that suggest the preference or highlight some new typeface that has been 'developed for dyslexics'. However, every attempt has been made through this book to ensure that all information is 'evidence-based', and the choice of typeface will be dealt with in the same fashion. For this reason, while it would be possible to apparently cover this topic in a few lines, a more in-depth analysis is provided. The reason is that all decisions should be informed, from the choice of which single typeface to use in a paper-based publication to the personal choices that should be available in an e-learning environment, whether it is a web page or CD-based learning.

> ### Terminology – typeface and font
>
> People often confuse the terms typeface and font, even though their definitions are clear. Typeface refers to the style or pattern of a set of letters (or characters). Parts that change can be thickness, roundness and how fancy (curly) they are. One common classification is 'serif' and 'sans serif', sometimes referred to as 'with feet' and 'without feet'. For example, look closely at the lines of text below. They are written in Times, and have little 'feet' on the bottom of the 'T' and 'h', as well as curls on the crossbar of the 'T'.
>
> Font refers to the parameters applied to the typeface. This can be characteristics such as bold and italic, as well as size (e.g., 12 point), leading (space between lines) and kerning (space between letters).

BDA publications

In 1995, the British Dyslexia Association (BDA) published *Dyslexia: Signposts to Success*. This was its first (and very successful) attempt at development of a self-help book for dyslexic individuals. That is, the target reader was dyslexic. In those days there were no options of an electronic version and therefore a single choice of a typeface had to be made. At the time (unfortunately no written reference has been found) the attitude within the dyslexia field was that the tops and tails of the 'serif' typefaces led the eye from one letter to another (i.e. it is a reflection of cursive handwriting), which made it easier for the dyslexic individual to read. Therefore, the choice of typeface for the 1995 book was Times New Roman.

The first major publication of the BDA to change its typeface was *Dyslexia Contact*, the tri-annual magazine of the organization. That was in 2000, and the choice was Arial. However, this was not the result of a lobby, widespread consultation or research, but a 'feeling' that, following a 'straw poll' the membership would prefer it. There were less than ten voices of appreciation when the typeface changed, and a few that lamented the loss of the 'comfort' of the old style. The *Dyslexia Handbook* changed its typeface in 2002, and the typeface used in the 2007/8 edition was Futura. It was argued that the rounded shape of the letter 'ɑ' is easier for the dyslexic user to read. However, it may also give visual confusion since it looks a bit like an 'o'. There is no dyslexia-specific research to support the choice.

In the BDA's *Dyslexia Handbook* 2008/9, 37 out of 48 (77 per cent) advertisers that specifically mentioned dyslexia used predominantly sans serif typeface in their advertisements. That means 23 per cent use predominantly serif typefaces!

Different typefaces

Here are some examples of different typefaces:

Some people like the widely available Arial (or Helvetica on Macs).

The Comic Sans has been accused of looking too child-like, yet many like it.

Tahoma is the typeface preferred by many dyslexic readers.

Trebuchet has a little more space between the letters.

Times New Roman is a traditional print choice, but not for websites.

Verdana has a more open feel and is a popular website choice.

Case study 5 Preferred typeface

A small piece of (unpublished) research was carried out by the author with the explicit intention of finding out what was the preferred typeface of the dyslexic reader. Some 80 severe dyslexic users were asked to read three pages of text. (NB This was paper-based and not on a computer.) The first page contained the instructions, while the other pages contained two stories, one in Arial and the other in Times. The Arial text was reduced slightly in size to make it appear to be the same size visually to the Times. Half the time story A was in Arial, and half the time in Times. The order of appearance of the stories and the typeface were carefully modified and recorded. In the end there appeared to be no difference between the two. However, there did appear to be one predictor, which was that whatever was used as the typeface for the Instructions became the preferred typeface for the test items. The tentative conclusion was that the reader will choose what they are used to. (NB The research remains unpublished as it was felt the size of the data set was insufficient for publication.)

This echoes Eric Gill's claim in *An Essay on Typography* (1931) that 'Legibility, in practice, amounts simply to what one is accustomed to.' Zuzana Licko, co-author with Rudy VanderLans of *Émigré: Graphic Design into the Digital Realm* (1994), repeated that assertion in suggesting that 'Typefaces are not intrinsically legible; rather, it is the reader's familiarity with faces that accounts for their legibility. Studies have shown that readers read best what they read most' (quote from www.caslon.com.au/readabilitynote2.htm).

Dyslexia-friendly typefaces

In the past, a number of individuals have attempted to make dyslexia-friendly fonts. Although they have to battle with the fact that every person has his or her own preferences, the 'research' has led to a greater understanding of what make a good typeface, although the limited uptake reminds us that the 'preference' is not just a matter of ease of reading and visual preference, but also wider availability, economics and what we are used to.

The typefaces here (and the references provided) offer a guide to alternative ways to investigate the concepts. High on the priorities of the designers is to ensure a clear distinction between the shape of each letter. Key areas include making a capital 'I' distinct from a lower case 'L', ensure a visual difference between the 'rounded' letters ('a', 'c', 'e' and 'o'), and maximize the difference between mirror letters such as 'b' and 'd', and 'p' and 'q'.

One of the most widely mentioned 'dyslexia' fonts is Read Regular, by the Dutch designer Natascha Frensch. She attempted to provide each letter with a distinctive character to avoid the traditional confusion due to similarity to be found in 'b', 'd', 'p' and 'q'. However, the differences remain by necessity subtle. That is, the designer has to conform to convention, and can only adjust the detail. Despite the widespread publicity of the typeface on the web in 2003, there is little sign of it being available. The website (www.readregular.com) still exists complete with examples, but there is no apparent way to purchase the font. However, one children's book company appears to be using it.

In 2007, Rob Hillier completed his PhD that involved development of a dyslexia-friendly font – sylexiad (www.robsfonts.com/sylexiadserif.html). His research included an investigation into the alternative forms, and his final version was documented as being the result of refinements through user feedback. However, like most dyslexia fonts, its uptake is going to be limited as it is necessary to buy the font.

K-Type created the Lexia font which they claim is dyslexia-friendly. They have made it available free for private use, although no statistics are available on whether dyslexic individuals do like it, or its level of uptake (www.k-type.com/fontlexia.html). According to their website, the strength of their font is the non-symmetrical form of their 'b' and 'd', as well as an 'a' and 'g' that are similar to handwritten forms which may help dyslexic readers.

Although not a 'dyslexia' font, another worthy of mention is Tiresias. This was commissioned by the Royal National Institute for the Blind (RNIB) as a suite of fonts to suit different occasions but especially for computer use. The PC font can be viewed at www.tiresias.org/fonts/pcfont/view_pc.htm. The big advantage is that they can be downloaded and used freely. Although better than having to buy the font, unless the font comes installed on the machine, the uptake will be limited (www.tiresias.org/fonts/fonts_download.htm). The commitment of the RNIB to their typeface is indicated by the fact that the default font for their web pages is Tiresias. This was not found with any other of the 'special' fonts.

The Sassoon typeface has been around for more than 20 years but, while many people quote it, few use it due to the relatively high cost. However, an excellent book on the background can be downloaded free at www.clubtype.co.uk/fonts/sas/Why%20Sassoon.pdf. Examples of the difference include the rounded 'a' (looking similar to an 'o'), the long tails of letters such as 'j' and 'y', and the long tail of the 'f' emulating the older handwriting style for this letter. According to Sassoon, these make the letters more distinct. However, there is no published research on its advantages, or why a rounded presentation of a letter such as '**ɑ**' is more distinct from the letter 'o' than the more conventional 'a'.

Case study 6 Online survey of fonts

The Davis website provided one of only a few examples of online font 'research', although they are more qualitative than quantitative (www.dyslexia.com/info/webdesign.htm). The website offered the following statistics (accessed 19 July 2008). However, there was no confirmation as to whether the users were dyslexic or not.

Which font face is easiest to read on a web page?

Arial (sans serif): 51.30%

Times Roman (serif): 26.92%

Something else: 15.02%

No preference: 6.76%

Total votes: 4,228

This is consistent with anecdotal reports.

Font size

With paper documents, it is necessary to fix the size of the text, and the font size will have an impact on the ecological footprint of the document, i.e. the number of pages and the cost. However, while the document remains in the electronic format (i.e. provided it is not printed), there are no such restrictions.

In relative terms, the slightly bigger font can be better for adults, and anecdotal evidence suggests also for dyslexic users. Research (Bernard et al. 2001a) found that for adults a 14-pt font was more legible, and led to faster reading than 12-pt fonts, but were preferred less than sans serif. They concluded that if reading speed was more important, then serif fonts should be used. But if the criterion were user preference, then sans serif should be the default.

However, Geske (www.public.iastate.edu/~geske/scholarship.html) carried out research on different on-screen font sizes, and comparing serif and sans serif fonts. He found that point sizes greater than 12 pt were preferred subjectively but led to a slower reading speed. However, comprehension as measured by short-term recall was found to be optimal at 12 pt, rather than the alternatives of 14 pt or 10 pt. Although Geske suggests this contradicts conventional wisdom, logic would suggest there must be an optimal size where things are most efficient. However, clearly visual preference and comprehension preferences, at least in this research, do not always coincide. Note that this was with non-dyslexic (or unknown) individuals, and the results may be different for dyslexic users.

The traditional way to control the font size in a website has been to have the designer set the default size, and then the user adjusts the size using the browser. However, increasingly designers (and web page specifiers) are building in simple accessibility tools whereby you click on a button available on the website (or through a Preferences button) and can instantly see the change in size of the body text. Unfortunately many websites set their defaults at too small a size for most dyslexic users. Furthermore, some still fail to allow easy adjustment (e.g., through the browser) with the consequence of not only disenfranchizing the users, but also arguably breaking disability legislation. This ability to change font size quickly and easily is important, as not only does everybody have different preferences but also the screen resolution will significantly affect the apparent size of the text on the screen.

It has even been suggested that fonts have personality traits (see, e.g., Shaikh et al. 2006). In 'Perception of fonts: perceived personality traits and uses' (www.surl.org/usabilitynews/81/PersonalityofFonts.asp), these authors analysed a whole series of fonts and used statistical methods to group the characteristics. While not generally important, the user should know that while a typeface such as Comic Sans may be easier to read, when receiving a document in this typeface many adults see it as childish, and it may not have the intended impact. Therefore the suggestion for dyslexic users with this preference is to compose using their preference, but to change just before sending.

Shaikh et al. (www.surl.org/usabilitynews/101/pof.asp) also talk about the perception of the reader in cases such as job applications, where the font choice would impact upon the interviewer's perceptions of the interviewee. (They suggested that in their choice of three for their research that Corbel was highly appropriate, Tempus Sans was 'neutral' and Vivaldi was 'inappropriate'.)

Another piece of quantitative research with respect to children (Bernard et al. 2001b) suggested that 14 pt was easier and quicker to read. Furthermore, in a comparison of Times New Roman, Courier, Arial and Comic Sans MS,

Comic Sans was seen as more attractive than the serif fonts, and Arial 14 pt and Comic Sans 12 pt were seen as the best:

This text has been written in Arial 14 pt.

This text has been written in Comic Sans 12 pt.

Finally, as a word of warning, Bernard et al. (2001c) highlighted due caution in their own research as the research was all carried out in the United States and this may not be applicable to international audiences. Therefore, all designers should carry out usability studies with the local user group. This again reflects the words of Gill and Licko mentioned above, that what counts is what you are used to.

Case study 7 Dystrain and fonts

Dystrain was a project run by the Welsh Dyslexia Project, in collaboration with colleagues in Sweden, Romania and Hungary. The aim was to understand the issues with respect to e-learning and the dyslexic individual. (There was also a by-product of an accredited e-learning course for teachers.) The project provides some evidence of the difference in preferences that distinguished between dyslexic and non-dyslexic individuals, although not in sufficient quantities to enable full statistical analysis. The results for the UK are as shown in Table 6.1.

Table 6.1 Font preferences

	Dyslexic users (%)	Non-dyslexic users (%)
Times	5	21
Courier	0	7
Comic Sans	69	42
Verdana/Arial	23	26
Other	3	2
Any	0	2

Clearly Comic Sans was the preferred typeface in both cases. However, the preference was more toward the sans serif for the dyslexic users, and it may be argued that the non-dyslexic users were not as concerned as to which was used.

Interestingly in Hungary, where there is not a tradition of being able to adjust personal preferences and nor such wide access to the internet as in the UK, results were that more than 50 per cent of dyslexic and 75 per cent of non-dyslexic users preferred Times, while figures of Arial were 27 per cent and 8 per cent respectively. (Comic Sans was not available.) Hungarian results suggest that familiarity is an important issue.

Kerning and ligature

Kerning refers to the space between letters. In Microsoft Word it may be found through the menus: Format/Font/Character spacing.

> The character spacing for this line is set at 100 per cent.
> The character spacing for this line is expanded by 0.5 pt.

A ligature is formed when two letters occur close together and become one character. The most common letter that has problems is 'f', especially before 'i'. This will depend upon the font in question, but a typical problem is the dot of the 'i' is lost in the top curve of the 'f'. Computers have ensured this happens less often by having automated adjustment of the lettering.

Case study 8 The importance of legibility

For an indication of the importance of legibility, the BBC in 2002 reported an incident of an air traffic controller who sent a Glasgow plane to Cardiff after misreading the small text on his screen. Apparently he misread EGPF (Glasgow) as EGFF (Cardiff). There are reports of other similar problems such as with aircraft heights, confusing FL360 (36,000ft) with FL300 (30,000ft) at small size. Apparently these problems have now been fixed, but it does offer a warning of the importance of getting it right!

Today the computer offers a wide range of possible alternatives, and any study skills support for the dyslexic individual should contain not only training on how to use assistive technology, but also how to change the typefaces, etc.

In the end, the preference is personal, and any 'settings' should, as far as possible, allow the individual to choose his or her own preference, whether it is serif, sans serif or any other characteristic. There is software that allows individuals to design their own typefaces (see, e.g., http://fontstruct.fontshop.com/ for free software or www.fontlab.com/ for commercial software).

Leading (line spacing)

Leading (rhymes with bedding) refers to the vertical space between lines and is now more commonly referred to as 'line spacing'. It derives from the days when letters were made of lead, and leading referred to the strips of lead put between lines to separate them. As well as simple aesthetic appeal, increased white space can help separate the descenders (as in 'g', 'j', 'p', 'q') from the ascenders (the parts of letter that rise up, such as in 'b', 'd', 'f', 'h', 'k', 'l', 't') which otherwise can blend together indistinguishably. In most programs, the line spacing default is set as a multiple of the size of the letters. This is because it allows the result to be seen as a ratio, and is therefore not affected by the magnification on the screen. It can also be set as a fixed number of 'points'.

Leading and readability

The text in the first paragraph from *Alice in Wonderland* is 12 pt with single spacing (12 pt), whereas the second is 12 pt with 16 pt (1.25) line spacing.

Alice was beginning to get very tired of sitting by her sister on the bank, and of having nothing to do: once or twice she had peeped into the book her sister was reading, but it had no pictures or conversations in it, 'and what is the use of a book,' thought Alice 'without pictures or conversation?'

So she was considering in her own mind (as well as she could, for the hot day made her feel very sleepy and stupid), whether the pleasure of making a daisy-chain would be worth the trouble of getting up and picking the daisies, when suddenly a White Rabbit with pink eyes ran close by her.

(Lewis Carroll, *Alice in Wonderland*)

Justification

Justification refers to the way the text sits between margins. Left justified will keep the text to the left, maintaining the regular spaces between words, creating a 'ragged right' edge. Right justified puts the wording up against the right margin, and creates a 'ragged left' margin. Fully justified spaces the sentence out across the full width of the page, putting gaps between the words to ensure the last letter of the last word on the line is right up against the margin. The consequence is to cause the spaces to be of irregular size. The result (according to anecdotal reports) is that the dyslexic reader can become confused about the boundary between words. Although this may be counter-intuitive, since adding extra space between words would appear to make it clear where word boundaries existed, this problem is widely reported.

As a rule, text should be left justified with a chance for the dyslexic user to see a jagged pattern down the right side which can help the location of areas that need to be re-read when returning to a page. If the entire right side looks similar, there are no easy markers.

Layout issues

Colours, layout and design

The main parameters to consider in layout and design are:

- text and background colour
- scrolling or paged content
- line length and columns
- headings
- use of 'white' space.

As with other aspects, much of the research is based on results of non-dyslexic individuals. However, there is also anecdotal evidence that can help design of web and e-learning layout.

Case study 9 Barrington Stoke

Barrington Stoke, a leading publisher of books for 'reluctant readers' allow its readers to help choose the typeface and font for their book. They work with focus groups that include many dyslexic children to see what they like and how they would prefer the text to appear. These groups also make suggestions about which words are 'in', and when some words are not clear.

In the early days, the font used was an adaptation of Cecilia, chosen because the shapes mirrored the handwritten shapes learned at school, in particular the 'a' and the 'g'. It also found that older readers and adults who have been exposed to print for longer chose more familiar typefaces such as Arial or Times.

It now uses a typeface designed specially for the company. However, leading and point size as well as the spacing after paragraphs differ depending on the target market (see Table 6.2).

Table 6.2 Spacing for different target markets

Target market	Font size	Leading	Gap between paragraphs
Reading age 8 (fiction for 8–12)	14	20	5mm
Reading age 8 (teen fiction)	13.5	17	3mm
Teenager with reading age of 7	14	28	8.7mm

There is no right-hand justification and there is an 8mm indent on the first line of every paragraph. Double quotation marks are used to signify dialogue, with single quotation marks used within a quotation (in UK mainstream publishing, single are generally used first, then double within). Whole words in capitals are avoided as poor readers find it difficult to read these words. The paper is chosen to have minimum text showing through from the other side, and is off-white, which is restful to the eye.

Text and background colour

Today's designer of websites has a whole range of controlling technology to optimize the learning environment. This includes Cascading Style Sheets, specialist programming such as php and asp, as well as programs like Adobe Flash. Together they offer many solutions to controlling all attributes of the interface, of which the background colour is the most conspicuous.

Google and the colour of money

It seems that Google has done some research on the response to subtle changes in the link colours in their adverts. Apparently a subtle change from a dull to a more vibrant blue increases the chance that you will click through to an advert. If Google can consider the impact of such subtle colour changes on the ability to perceive information, it is not such a leap to understand how using the preferred colours could help the dyslexic learner.

Website for discovering your preferences

At the website www.wdnf.info/colours/en/ you can change the background colour, font colour, typeface, line spacing and even the gaps between letters. At the end you can print your results. It is hoped that the research on this website will inform design through evidence-based results. Similar studies are being carried out in Chinese, Portuguese, Hungarian and Bulgarian.

There is little doubt that the ability to change the background to one's preferred colour can have a tremendous impact on the dyslexic individual, although the research to prove it is minimal. The reason is that everybody is different, and the results need to be considered with due deference to perceived preference, reading speed and reading comprehension.

The Web Accessibility Initiative (WAI)

The Web Accessibility Initiative has provided some guidelines with respect to colour combinations. However, its work is geared towards provision for the blind user. As discussed in Chapter 9, this can be clearly seen in their website, which is a poor exemplar for those looking to design accessible websites. Earlier versions of their recommendations included a high contrast level, which may have been inappropriate for many dyslexic individuals. More recently they have relented towards a user-led approach.

Case study 10 Background colour research

There are a few examples of colour background research, although they are more qualitative than quantitative. For example, the Davis website (www.dyslexia.com/info/webdesign.htm) offers the following statistics (Table 6.3) (accessed 19 July 2008).

Table 6.3 Which background colour is best for a web page?

Colour	(%)
White	29.64
Cream	20.86
Blue	19.68
Green	7.80
Black	7.73
No Preference	5.92
Gray	4.25
Something Else	4.11
Total Votes	2,871

Although this appears to contradict BDA and the Adult Dyslexia Organization (ADO) advice, it should be noted that there was no differentiation between dyslexics and non-dyslexic users.

Drop-down menus

Many sites offer a drop-down menu, where colours are displayed. This means the user can click on the colour they want and change the page accordingly. Unfortunately these changes apply only to the background colour, and may cause some of the design elements to be lost. If there is a header in blue and the body text is black, to change the background colour to blue would mean the header could no longer be seen. For this reason, template-based colour changes are preferable. Try the ones on the BDA (www.bdadyslexia.org.uk) or EMBED (www.embeddyslexia.eu) websites.

Browser modifications

Many websites simply suggest that the user goes to the browser to make the changes. This is always an option, but few people know about it. The method is very useful for the partially sighted, but the loss of the design elements can make it difficult for the dyslexic user, especially if text box colours are overwritten.

Others have a limited range of colour backgrounds, such as yellow on black, or white on black as favoured by the visually impaired community. The design limitations placed on the website by having a unique background colour suggest that the approach used by the Texdic, which offers a series of templates (i.e. fixed combinations of colours to avoid colour clashes) provides a better solution. Another alternative is a small graphic showing a background colour with a central circle indicating the text colour can be found at the EU-funded project EMBED (www.embeddyslexia.eu).

Colour blindness

Approximately 5–8 per cent of the male population (and 0.5 per cent of females) have some form of colour blindness with the perception of red or green being most often affected. www.vischeck.com/vischeck/vischeckURL.php provides a method to see if the colour combinations used will cause difficulties for those with colour blindness. (NB It does not work on all websites.)

Discussions of colours should not stop with website development. There are also e-learning environments, presentations, documents produced by others and those produced by the dyslexic individual, and all of the documents produced in Microsoft Office and Open Office. Do not be limited to what your computer dictates, play around with the browser and the fonts and colours until you find the best one for you.

Background colours in Word

It is easy to change the background colour in Word when you are working on-screen. It can be accessed in Format > Background. You can then turn off the colour when printing or sending it to somebody.

Background colour – Acrobat Reader

We tend to think of pdfs being presented in a fixed format. But fortunately Adobe is well aware of accessibility issues. Not only does it provide a built in text-to-speech system but also allows you to change background colours.

In order to change the background colour of a pdf in Acrobat Reader, go to Edit > Preferences > Accessibility, and check 'Replace document colours'. Click 'Page Background' to change to your preferred colour.

Changing browser settings

Browsers offer a number of accessibility functions which address the main areas of:

- font size
- colour combination
- typeface.

Font size

You can change the font size through the browser in two ways:

1. By magnifying everything through the use of Ctrl + + (and Ctrl + -).
2. By modifying the browser settings through Tools > Options > Content.

Background colours

This can be changed through Tools > Options > Content. It provides the option to override the designer setting.

Line length and columns

The conventional wisdom on line length for printed material is a maximum of 80 characters per line. However, there are mixed reports about the line lengths for use on monitors. According to Shaikh (2005), some research suggests that longer line lengths of 80 to 100 characters per line (cpl) while others found that 55 characters per line were read faster than either 100 cpl or 25 cpl conditions. Other research suggested that adults preferred medium line lengths (76 cpl) while children preferred shorter line lengths (45 cpl) when compared with 132 cpl. Reading times for the same amount with text were the same, irrespective of the column width, possibly because the increased speed of reading the shorter line length was offset by the need to scroll.

Note that, if columns are used, the dyslexic individual prefers to have some sort of solid indicator of the difference between the columns, such as a simple thin line that separates the columns. This ensures the reader does not simply cross from one column to the next while reading.

Scrolling or paged content

Consideration should be given to whether information should be given on a page-by-page basis, as in a book, or through scrolling. Once again there is no research with respect to the dyslexic user, and the research for general users is mixed. In 1998, Dyson and Kipping found that users could read paged content faster than scrolled, with no difference between the two on comprehension. However, further research by Baker (2003) suggests the scrolling can be quicker. This, he speculated, was because the idea of scrolling had become a more familiar concept to the proficient users in software such as Word as well as on the internet. Also, it was suggested that when you wanted to go back and forth in text (as many dyslexic users would want to do), it was much easier in scrolled text than paged.

Use of 'white' space

The use of white space is not widely researched, and the information with respect to dyslexic users is only from feedback from those who have participated in focus groups, or comment on layout in other contexts. Research by Chaparro et al. (2004) suggests that for non-dyslexic readers, reading was slower when margins were available, but comprehension was better with margins. However, it is difficult to be clear if line length was a confound to this result since it appears total width (including the margins) was constant.

They reported that leading did not affect the performance, but eye strain was less with increased leading. They also reported that the font 'looked bigger' with the increased leading and was preferred. For the dyslexic user, the use of white space can be important as it helps separate parts of the information. The increased leading helps to separate lines, and especially keeps apart the risers and descenders that otherwise could interfere with each other as discussed earlier.

Some people advise that for dyslexic readers the gap should be 1.5 lines, or 18 pt for a 12-pt text. However, experience shows (e.g., in the research for the Barrington Stoke range of books) that by making the space between lines too big, the reader becomes uncomfortable as they have to try to follow on from one line to the next, and the sense is lost. On paper, the dyslexic reader is able to use a ruler or similar tool. But on screen the problem is solvable but more difficult.

On-screen colours

There are a number of ways you can change the overall 'feel' of the computer working environment by adjusting the colours. These include changing the system settings (colours, fonts and sizes) through the Control Panel, using specialist software (e.g., ReadAble from Iansyst) or using the functionality that may occur within other software (e.g., the screen colour option in Screen Ruler Suite from Claro Software).

Ten tips about preferences

1. Where the e-learning environment can be changed, change it.
2. Provide feedback to designers and content managers about the dyslexia-friendly nature (or not!) of their website.
3. Where modifications cannot be made in the learning environment, see if it can be copied and pasted into another program such as Microsoft Word.
4. Talk to other users of the program.
5. For chat and messaging, try composing in Microsoft Word (with their spellchecker) and then copying the message into the chat zone.
6. If the site is password protected, make sure it is written down in several obvious places.
7. Make printouts wherever possible. These are often easier to annotate.
8. Use text-to-speech to access the content, if necessary copying the text into another environment.
9. If it does not work, do not assume that it is only you that has the problem.
10. Do not assume that everything has to be done using the computer.

Preferred view in the browser

There are two ways you can influence the preference in the browser. You can use the settings to change size, colours, fonts, etc. as mentioned above. But you can also change the layout for web searches. The traditional search provides a stream of text that needs a lot or reading to interpret. However, there are some 'search engines' that provide a more dyslexia-friendly version.

There are a number of Add-ons for Mozilla Firefox that make it more dyslexic-friendly. These include Foxtab which allows you to layout all those browsers you have open at the same time in one browser page, so that you can choose the right one; CoolPreview, which helps display information, while Transferr, Sthrt and homepagestartup are all visually-based home page management sites.

Conclusion

Given the freedom that is now possible through computers, it is time for the dyslexic user to stand up and be counted. It is easy for those working in the dyslexia field to point out examples of good practice. But the fact that one can highlight good practice does not mean it is universal.

Not everybody is prepared to wait. Two US-based law suits highlight the complexity of issues, if not in dyslexia at least in the disability field.

A US online store was successfully prosecuted for failing to implement web functionality so that all users (i.e. visually impaired shoppers) would have an equal opportunity to buy goods from the website. As the consequence, their website has changed. This was a fairly easy to understand issue.

The second related to a university in the US attempting to implement the use of Amazon's e-book Kindle as part of course practice. It came unstuck when one visually impaired student said he was unable to access the content as the functions of the device were not made for visually impaired individuals. He complained that therefore he would have to wait several weeks while appropriate material was made for him. Unfortunately, the consequence is that many universities may not take up the dyslexic-friendly Kindle, with its talking books. Some argue that the student should have been targeting the real problem, which was the ongoing issue of the delay to him having access to course work. That has always been there, and always been an unacceptable discrimination. It is unfortunate that the dyslexia-friendly Kindle becomes a target for highlighting the issue and, rather than being widely implemented and used by many dyslexic individuals, may find that it is not used, and everybody continues to suffer from delays in making coursework accessible.

Universal design, if ever it could be achieved, is a long way off. Fortunately we now have the tools to enable dyslexic users to adapt their interface to their needs. However, before we do that, we need: (1) to know the potential; and (2) to ensure designers and specifiers include the capabilities for change, preferably before anybody has to resort to disability legislation to make them.

7

E-learning and Knowledge Assessment

Introduction

There are two sides to learning: the acquisition of knowledge, and the verification that learning has taken place. This chapter looks at the role of the technology with respect to e-learning for dyslexic individuals, and the use of computers in examinations.

E-learning usually refers to the acquisition of learning through an electronic medium and should be seen as part of the blended learning that involves not only the electronic format, but also working with peers, tutors and traditional (paper-based) material. However, the environment also has an impact on the outcomes (learning acquired, speed of learning and efficiency) and, although not well researched, there is anecdotal evidence that dyslexic individuals feel more comfortable learning in an environment they can control and adapt so that each component fits their comfort zone. It is not about likes or dislikes, but a consideration of the components such as e-tutors (i.e. tutors who are using technology to support rather than face-to-face), chat, accessibility and usability, learning structure, use of multimedia, etc.

Computer-based (or other electronic device) assessment of learning is still a relatively new science that (like e-learning) owes much of its history to the technologists rather than the educationalists. Developments are now mature enough to be considered for wider uptake, including high stakes testing. However, there is still little research which looks at the specific problems faced by dyslexic individuals.

We will not review the vast diversity of learning software that is currently available since it is so diverse and evolving so rapidly that to try to truly offer a 'state of the art' snapshot would be out of date even before publication. Instead the key areas will be discussed specifically within the context of the impact upon the dyslexic individual in order to understand how to make decisions, how to interpret research, how to improve the system, and how to improve support.

Note that the issues of accessibility, usability and the user interface are more fully discussed in Chapter 6.

That said, the technology can provide an opportunity for individualization, and can support the dyslexic student who otherwise will remain floundering in the classroom since the other students in the class will have moved so far beyond him or her that they have disengaged from the activity. (There are still many teachers who refuse to allow dyslexic pupils to 'withdraw' from a lesson so they can, for example, practise basic skills using appropriate software, because they believe the child will 'fall behind even further'. That is, the teacher fails to appreciate that the child is already disengaged and not learning, so withdrawing will certainly not put him or her behind. And if he or she is provided with appropriate technological support, he or she may even improve!)

In order to understand the scope of the problem, let us consider a few examples where the demands and difficulties of the dyslexic individual have not been considered. (NB Note that these issues have been found in e-learning for dyslexics of all ages.)

1. A business management course designed for the self-employed who probably did not have university education. The test questions were well above university level and would have been difficult for dyslexics to access due to the reading level, rather than content.
2. Overzealous designers and technologists provide animation just because they can, rather than adding to the pedagogical dimension. Although they may think it adds to understanding, the additions simply make it more confusing and distracting for dyslexic users as well as others.
3. A widely used e-learning environment was analysed for the number of clickable areas. More than 50 hot spots were found that were visible on one screen. This means that not only is there not much working area but also there is visual confusion and a good chance of going to the wrong area accidentally.
4. A live chat zone was included as a compulsory part of a course, i.e. it would be assessed as part of the overall course result. The chat had no potential to set preferences for text size or font, nor background colour. Of greater significance was the lack of a spellchecker.

Despite these potential negatives, there are good reasons why the dyslexic learner can enjoy the e-learning environment. The main reasons are the degree of anonymity, and the potential for the user to control the learning, being able to pace yourself, set personal preferences, hide one's errors and access all information through text-to-speech can provide considerable confidence. and can reduce stress levels for the dyslexic learner. However, this assumes the e-learning environment can allow this.

Legal issues

But before we consider how e-learning can be both disabling and enabling, let us consider the legislation that pertains to these issues and where responsibility should lie. It may be argued, particularly under the UK Special Educational Needs Disability Act, that the problem is solely with the provider of the e-learning. While this may be the case, it is also important to take responsibility for one's own learning. What is equally important, but has not filtered through to those who are developing the courses, is that everybody is different and would like their machine to be set up in a way that is particular to them. This is especially true of dyslexic individuals who are less tolerant than others to set-ups outside their personal preference.

Across Europe, legislation has been implemented that seeks to limit discrimination in education and the workplace. The following quote is taken from the UK Disability Discrimination Act (DDA), and is representative of what can be found in other countries.

> A person has a disability if he has a physical or mental impairment which has a substantial and long-term adverse effect on his ability to carry out normal day-to-day activities.

The legislation goes on to define discrimination in two ways: (1) Discrimination occurs when someone is refused or deliberately not provided with service; provided with a lower standard of service; or service in a poorer manner; or provided with service on poorer terms than other people are treated, and this treatment cannot be justified. (2) It also occurs when a service provider fails, without justification, to make a reasonable adjustment.

Thus, from a legal perspective, it could be suggested that an e-learning environment contravenes legislation if:

1. Somebody is refused entry to a course because he or she is dyslexic (e.g., a tutor refuses a person entry to a language course because he or she thinks it will be too difficult for the student).
2. If the content was modified for the dyslexic individual, and this led to a lower quality.
3. If the dyslexic individual is assessed for something that measures his or her disability rather than his or her ability.

Furthermore, consideration should be given to the interpretation of 'provided with services on poorer terms'. If the 'terms' of the education are to provide learning in an accessible manner (even if this is implicit), then unless reasonable adjustments are made for the dyslexic individual, e.g. provision of text-to-speech, then it may be considered against the law. This legislation, it may be argued, will apply to all aspects of e-learning, which includes multimedia CDs used on stand-alone devices, intranet courses and resources as well as anything downloaded through the internet. Thus it includes both local and distance learning.

Pedagogy and construction of e-learning

Pedagogy refers to the framework for teaching and learning employed in a given environment, which should be based on sound evidence-based practices. E-learning developers attempt to address the principles of learning using conventional methods, and adapt them to the individualized environment of the computer. In order to provide a theoretical setting for e-learning, much of which can be contextualized to the dyslexic individual, Nichols, in his (2003) article 'Theory for eLearning', suggested a series of hypotheses to provide a framework for the interaction between the educational and technological components of e-learning. These were then adapted to reflect the needs of the dyslexic individual (Smythe 2004) and are given below, in an updated form.

Hypothesis 1

> E-learning is a means of implementing education that can be applied within varying education models (e.g., face-to-face or distance education) and educational philosophies (e.g., behaviourism and constructivism).

But the needs of dyslexics may exceed those of other individuals. They have a lower tolerance to parameters outside their comfort zone such as background colours and text layout. There should be enough flexibility to ensure everyone, including the dyslexic learner, can adopt an approach to learning that offers the greatest potential for success.

Hypothesis 2

> E-learning enables unique forms of education that fits within the existing paradigms of face-to-face and distance education.

E-learning may provide the way to manipulate the context and interface to the needs of the dyslexic individual more than the human-based alternatives such as tutors and lecturers. But there is no need to limit the use to existing paradigms. The technology itself may generate new ones.

Hypothesis 3

> The choice of e-learning tools, including assistive technology, should reflect rather than determine the pedagogy of a course. How the technology is used is often more important than which technology is used.

Put another way, there are many functions of assistive technology that could benefit the dyslexic that are not used because nobody knows they exist. (And dyslexic individuals will generally not read instruction manuals. The language used in most user manuals is incomprehensible even to non-dyslexic individuals.)

Hypothesis 4

E-learning advances primarily through the successful implementation of pedagogical innovation.

If it does not work well, it will not be used in future. Furthermore, what is good for dyslexics is good for everyone, and widespread implementation of what works well with dyslexics can benefit others. E-learning will also advance if greater attention is paid to those who do not thrive in such learning environments.

Hypothesis 5

E-learning can be used in two major ways: the presentation of educational content, and the facilitation of educational processes.

Both aspects involve the way information is accessed, which is key to learning for dyslexic individuals. It involves not only the user interface but also integration of multimedia into the overall structure.

Hypothesis 6

E-learning tools are best made to operate within a carefully selected and optimally integrated course design model.

The e-learning tool should be designed for the case in hand, and not necessarily be seen as a tool for all situations. The learning preferences for the dyslexic individual may change with the content and should be adaptable as required.

Hypothesis 7

E-learning tools and techniques should be used only after consideration has been given to online versus offline trade-offs.

E-learning is not good for all dyslexics. Some dyslexics may prefer additional support, while others prefer the anonymity. As technology and access advance, the distinction between online and offline will decrease. The major advantage of online is the rapid deployment of software changes which may be advantageous to the dyslexic learner. This may be because (1) they do not have to do anything such as implement updates, and (2) imperfect systems can be made more dyslexia-friendly quickly and effectively as feedback is provided.

Hypothesis 8

Effective e-learning practice considers the ways in which end-users will engage with the learning opportunities provided to them.

The dyslexic may have greater difficulties in engaging with the learning environment due to prior learning experiences. Access to an appropriate focus group is important in the development of e-learning tools as they are matched to specific courses.

Hypothesis 9

The overall aim of education, that is, the development of the learner in the context of a predetermined curriculum or set of learning objectives, does not change when e-learning is applied.

However, e-learning may make it more accessible to the dyslexic learner for many reasons (see the four principles on p. 146).

Hypothesis 10

Only pedagogical advantages will provide a lasting rationale for implementing e-learning approaches.

If dyslexic individuals can be shown to learn by using these methods, they can be used by others. It is important to re-align thinking from the mass-production mode of traditional education to the individualized potential of e-learning. There may well be occasions when the e-learning approach used for the dyslexic learner is not the optimal approach for all. The importance is flexibility at the personal level.

In these hypotheses are a series of statements that are the focus of this chapter, namely, the way the dyslexic individual responds to e-learning, and the way in which it should be adapted in order to ensure maximum accessibility.

These changes are not as earth-shattering as they may at first appear. However, it can be argued that these hypotheses re-align the content to the learner, and decrease the focus on the technology and the often over-elaborate design. That is, designers like their products to look good. But this is often at the expense of the user. But returning control to the user does not mean reducing the aesthetics, it simply means more effort should be made to remember the user.

Case study 11 Calldysc (Collaborative Additional Language Learning for Dyslexic Schoolchildren)

This project set out to identify the potential to use mobile technology to motivate dyslexic school kids in Bulgaria, Hungary, Romania and Sweden to learn English. Or to put it another way – learn English on a mobile phone. The principle was to test two hypotheses:

1. Hypothesis 1 – It is possible to use the mobile phone with special needs children as the medium for learning a second language.
2. Hypothesis 2 – It is possible to use Web 2 principles as a learning and motivational aid to re-engage SEN children in language learning.

The project was a resounding success, with dyslexic youths in all countries enthusiastically not only embracing the technology as a learning medium, but also demonstrating through pre- and post-testing their learning over the brief testing period.

However, it would be wrong to suggest that Web 2 is a boon to dyslexic individuals, as it depends on the use (see later in this chapter).

As a result of the work in the Calldysc project and other experience, the author reinterpreted Nichol's hypotheses to create the following four principles (Györfi and Smythe 2009). Although they were developed from experiences with dyslexic learners, the principles apply to everybody. A brief annotation has been provided to show the impact for dyslexic individuals.

Principle 1

The aims and objectives of education should not change with the introduction of the technology. However, the speed and manner in which the aims and objectives are met may change.

> Technology can be empowering, and speed up (or slow down) the process. However, the end goals should be the same. That said, the goals can be changed by the technology, allowing more to be done within the timescale.

Principle 2

The choice of educational tools (software and hardware) should reflect the needs of the context (geographical, economic, cultural and educational), and not determine the outcome. How technology is used is more important than which technology is used.

> Just because it works in one place or a given learning context does not mean it will work in others, due not only to the technology, but also many other considerations. Most importantly, how the dyslexic individual is supported is crucial.

Principle 3

Share and learn from mistakes, share ideas and innovation, work collaboratively. Do not assume that the user must have made a mistake as the programmer cannot always anticipate every eventuality.

> Many dyslexic individuals have suffered for many years from failure. As a consequence, all too often when something does not work as it should do, it is seen as a personal failure. However, many dyslexic individuals are highly creative, and it is not that they cannot find the solution, but that they can find alternative solutions the developers had not anticipated. If more programmers used dyslexic focus groups, they would end up with more robust software.

Principle 4

The tools chosen should be seen as a supplement to classroom practice and not a replacement. Do not assume that the learning experience on a computer can be the same as with human intervention. Teachers should understand what is being taught.

Blended learning is the key, getting a right mix between the technology and the human components. User interfaces and help menus make assumptions about the user. The dyslexic learner has a more rigidly defined comfort zone when it comes to preferences. These may rapidly change as the learning changes. It will be a long time before the technology can adapt to the ever-changing needs of the dyslexic learner, both in terms of presentation and background information of learning. Until that time (if it ever comes), the dyslexic learner will always work best when there is human support available.

All of this reinforces Marshall McLuhan's (1964) idea that the manner in which content is delivered by the technology affects the perception and learning ('the medium is the message'). He went further to suggest that the medium can be more important than the content. It may be argued that he could be referring to future education, where the only 'content' that matters will be the need to know how to gather information through the internet. That is, the skill (and personal advantage) are not in knowledge retention as in the past but in understanding and using the most effective methods of knowledge retrieval.

> **Work skills**
>
> Many dyslexic individuals become very adept at information retrieval strategies since these can help overcome memory deficits. The problem is that while this skill may be a premium in business, in order to get into a job where those skills can be demonstrated, you first need to pass conventional exams, where the possibility of using those skills is minimal.

E-learning environments

There are two types of learning: synchronous and asynchronous learning. Synchronous means that, for example, when a teacher or tutor is talking to the camera, the student is watching at the same time in a different place. Asynchronous means the student and teacher do not have to be in their respective locations at the same time.

Although some people prefer synchronous learning, this method does remove the advantage of 'anytime' learning, since you have to attend at a fixed time. Not surprisingly the market share of synchronous e-learning dropped from 16 per cent in 2005 to 8 per cent in 2008. Software to support synchronous learning is similar to that now standard in web-conferencing software, since functionality is similar. The key components are:

- document sharing/presentation area (e.g., for PowerPoint presentations)
- desktop sharing
- participants list
- whiteboard
- chat area
- webcam and sound
- recording capabilities.

In addition, there may be quizzes, polls and other forms of interaction.

Examples of web conferencing include Elluminate, Dimdim and the Open University's FlashMeeting. However, some people prefer to use stand-alone tools, mixing components such as Skype and shared environments such as those available through online software such as Google Docs (Office), Editgrid (spreadsheet) and Scribblar (whiteboard).

 Author's Choice: I prefer using Dimdim, as it is versatile and does not require download and installations.

For the dyslexic user, the introduction of individual components can be less intimidating than trying to provide a system that does everything since the independent systems allow skills to be mastered at an appropriate pace. The integrated version can then be introduced at a later date. Note that the bigger the screen, the easier it is to handle these shared environments. Most crucially it often depends on somebody showing them how the first time by watching over their shoulder, and not through the computer.

As in a 'normal' learning environment, the most important aspect is the ability to revisit the 'scene' at a later date through some form of recording mechanism. This may be through the sound and visual components as well as shared components such as whiteboards.

The dyslexic member of an open synchronous learning environment may be reluctant to use the chat area, but if webcam facilities are available this should not be too important. (NB Currently most of these shared environments do not have spellcheckers. However, if the speed of the chat is not too fast, it would be possible to compose in Microsoft Word and then transfer the text to the chat.)

The other issue is one of interrupting the lecture. In a lecture theatre/classroom, it is easy to turn to one's buddy to ask a point of clarification. This is not possible in lecture environments. However, some students have found creative ways around this, such as running Skype in the background for separate conversations out of the 'class' system.

Once the principles have been understood and are widely used, they should be advantageous to the dyslexic user, since they offer the key function of being able to record everything that was said and link it directly to learning objects such as presentations, third party websites, etc. However, in the same way that lecturers had to retrain to think more visually to suit the diversity of learners in their courses, so too there will be an element of retraining as they embrace the new technologies, and avoid trying to repeat a standard lecture design for a lecture theatre directly through the computer.

Note that there are several types of shared e-learning environments. Some are of a 'broadcast' nature, where the 'lecturer' teaches and cannot be interrupted. Others are where one person is in control (normally the teacher but sometimes a moderator). The alternative is where the control is shared. These environments take some getting used to, and there should be appropriate rules and etiquettes set out initially so that nobody can dominate a session, and nobody sits in the background without doing anything (lurking).

Asynchronous e-learning refers to any e-learning that occurs without somebody else interacting at the same time, and is the dominant form of e-learning. It is the real advantage of e-learning – anytime learning. The issues around asynchronous learning are very similar to those of any computer-based environment, as discussed in Chapter 6. The environment is built in such a way that memory is not such an issue as all aspects can be revisited at any time. Over and above that, it is composed of structural sequential multisensory methods that can be modified to the needs of the individual (and not fixed by the assumptions of the developer).

Accessibility of text is crucial, whether it is CD or internet-based. Although most courses are now accessible in terms of being readable by text-to-speech software (thanks to the lobbying of the sight-impaired community), still little testing has been carried out with dyslexic user groups. Consequently, many dyslexic users still feel intimidated in e-learning environments as early difficulties remind them of failure in traditional classroom environments. Furthermore, there can be a greater feeling of isolation, which may not benefit all dyslexic individuals. In these cases the role of support, human and web-based, can be crucial.

Case study 12 Dystrain Project survey

Dystrain gave us some interesting insights into personal preferences among dyslexic individuals. In order to evaluate different forms of tutorial support, each participant in the survey was asked for their preferences. Results suggest that both dyslexic and non-dyslexic individuals preferred face-to-face individual tuition above all other possibilities, reminding us that technology is good, but cannot replace the personal touch.

For remote support, the results (number = 82 individuals, half of whom were dyslexic) showed that non-dyslexics and mildly dyslexic individuals preferred email to phone or webcam. However, the mildly and severely dyslexic individual preferred webcams. The email preference may be understood in terms of having a record to refer back to. Webcams can be useful if you don't like to read the words, and need visual cues to understand the answers, as in the case of the severely dyslexic individuals. Mildly dyslexic individuals like the visual clues, but did not feel they needed the recording.

When it comes to the way individuals respond, the research from Dystrain suggests that the pattern of preferences between dyslexic and non-dyslexic individuals is similar. Few wanted long essays, and there was a slight preference towards multiple choice as opposed to short open-ended answers.

Learning support

Who knows what tomorrow's technology may bring? But currently we can list five main types of support that are available for individual or group support. These are:

- email
- forums
- chat and conferencing
- blogging and micro-blogging
- shared environments.

The four main types of interaction between students and teachers/tutors are forums, chat, email and blogging. Each has its own advantages and disadvantages as far as the dyslexic individual is concerned.

Email

This is the commonest form, and has been discussed elsewhere. The advantages include:

- It is a well-established method of communication.
- It is usually private and one-to-one.
- One can compose elsewhere, using grammar checkers and spellcheckers.
- There is no time pressure.
- Answers are saved.
- It is easily accessed.
- The software can synchronize with other systems such as calendars.

Examples include: Microsoft Outlook and Outlook Express and Mozilla Thunderbird.

Forums

A forum refers to a collective of individuals who contribute to the overall knowledge of the group. This can be used to ask questions, share experiences and provide answers. These groups are generally dyslexia-friendly as they are asynchronous. That is, they are spread over time and there is no urgency. Therefore dyslexic individuals can compose an email in another environment such as Word, and then transfer it into their email. They can even send it to a friend first to check. Not only are they able to hide any reading and writing difficulties, they can also hide how long it took to write. For example, it would not be unusual for a dyslexic individual to take two hours to write, check, re-check and send an email that somebody else may take less than ten minutes to do.

The role of forums has changed over the past five years and their uptake will depend on how useful they can be. The good advice that previously was only available through peers and experts on forums is now widely available through the internet. The increasing power of semantic information extraction makes the information far more useful than in the past. As a consequence, forums are on the decline.

Dyslexic individuals prefer the type whereby the messages are sent directly to their email, rather than via a specific website. Apart from the general convenience, especially in this day and age of BlackBerries and continuous email through the mobile phone, it means there is no need (1) to remember to go to the site, and (2) to remember even more login names and passwords.

Some lecturers, particularly in America, have tried using forums not only for (closed) discussion groups but also as an assessable component for courses but with limited success. Most course directors would see this as contravening disability discrimination legislation by disadvantaging dyslexic individuals, and often attempting to assess skills that are not relevant to the knowledge base.

There are a number of forums with different focuses which can easily be found through an internet search. They can be good for self-help and research.

Chat and conferencing

Chat usually refers to typing short messages and talking through video either on a one-to-one basis, or in a group. Although there is the immediacy, if the group has been together for some time, they will usually know of the issues of the dyslexic members. Widespread use of broadband means that videos are a realistic option, especially when so many laptops come with integral webcams.

If the 'conversation' is restricted to text only, the dyslexic individual is disadvantaged since few systems have built-in spellcheckers, with the consequence that the dyslexic individual is hampered in expressing themselves when the chat is restricted to text. This means dyslexic individuals have two realistic options: (1) to type a message hoping their spelling and grammar are good enough and send it; or (2) to compose the message in a program where they can check spelling and grammar, such as Microsoft Word. If they go for option (1), they are in danger of not being understood, or even ridiculed in public. If they go for option (2), the conversation may have moved on by the time the person returns.

Furthermore, the working environment cannot always be adjusted to the user's needs. For example, not all chat systems allow the background colour to be changed. Again the main option would be to compose in another environment as mentioned above. Fortunately most now have provision for making the text larger, using a different font, and changing the font colour. But the main difficulty has not been addressed.

Examples of chat systems include: AOL Instant Messenger, Google Talk, ICQ, Skype, Windows Live Messenger and Yahoo! Messenger. If these systems are to be used effectively, recording should be integral to the user's experience. Although most chat has integral history storage, external systems are usually required for sound and video-based recording. (See Chapter 4 for examples.)

Numbers of chat users

The three leading global services (in terms of number of registered persons) are Windows Live Messenger with 330 million, Skype 309 million and Yahoo! Messenger 248 million. By comparison, the Chinese Tencent QQ has 320 million active users with over 40 million online at one time. National versions include Gadu-Gadu with 6 million users in Poland and MXit with 9 million users in South Africa. (Source: http://en.wikipedia.org/wiki/Instant_messaging)

Blogging and micro-blogging

Web 2 is about the user changing the web. Although some institutions have experimented with blogging as a support mechanism for students, this is not considered to be mainstream. That said, the wider availability of Content Management Systems means that tutors have greater access to management of their own online information including student support.

However, increasingly students and academics are turning to micro-blogging, of which the best known is Twitter. Although in its early days the system was used for little more than 'This is what am I doing now', there are strong signs of it maturing into a useful environment. Examples of how Twitter is now used for educational support include reminders of assignment deadlines, information updates (e.g., if a new book has been published) and shared experiences (e.g., when students want help in a specific area). These can be one-way (tutor to student) or as group communications. They have the advantage for dyslexics of being brief (under 140 characters), and nobody worries about the spelling as novel letter combinations are used to convey information with minimal characters. However, this can be a problem for those trying to use text-to-speech software, unless there is a chance to train it. The instant access, especially through the mobile phone, suggests that in future this could be an integral part of the support system. Examples of micro-blogging include: Twitter, Plurk and Jaiku.

Shared environments

Traditionally the tutor has offered not only the opportunity to talk but also to discuss work in progress. This includes spreading the work out in front to review it. Shared environments do not claim to be the same, but they do offer the potential for the support tutor and the dyslexic individual to look at the same work at the same time. These working environments may be simple online document collaboration (e.g., two people editing text at the same time). However, more sophisticated versions exist which as well as text chat, audio and video conferencing as standard also include the ability to collaborate on documents (documents, presentations, spreadsheets, whiteboards, etc.), as well as online web pages and the ability to record events while online.

The software used will be similar to those highlighted above under synchronous learning.

> ### Who owns a lecture?
>
> According to copyright specialist Dr Miglena Molhova, the law in Europe is different from that in the UK. Specifically, she notes that a dyslexic person, if recognized as a person with disabilities, can make records of a lecture even without asking for permission from the copyright holder, because he/she makes this for personal use and not for production or selling purposes. And even if not recognized as a person with disabilities, in most EU countries you are allowed to perform certain actions without payment and without asking the copyright holders when it comes to personal use. In most EU countries the copyright holder is usually the author (as opposed to the employer in the UK).

E-assessment of knowledge

Let us start by asking, why do we have examinations? The main answer is to demonstrate skill acquisition, and that a minimum standard has been reached. This may be in a variety of contexts, including the academic context such as passing an exam (GCSE, baccalaureate, degree or other level of competence) and demonstrating professional competence. The development and use of computer-based knowledge assessment with the general population have been widely documented elsewhere. Therefore comments here will concentrate on issues related to the dyslexic individual.

The UK Disability Discrimination Act (DDA) (and similar legislation around the world) as discussed above, clearly states that the ability and not the disability should be measured. However, the interpretation of rules is often done locally, and there is no consistency. We will not attempt to judge what is right or wrong, but merely highlight the 'alternatives' that have been implemented in recent years through a series of case studies.

Most examinations now come with two components – coursework and a final exam. There is little doubt that coursework is usually good news for dyslexic individuals since they can spread the load over a long time and not end up panicking in an exam, forgetting everything, and being removed from the comfort zone of their usual technology. They have the opportunity to use all their assistive technology, such as research and referencing aids, text-to-speech for background reading, summarizing software, concept mapping for planning and speech-to-text for writing. Online and offline spelling and grammar checkers help with the 'proofreading' component.

Examples of the software are given in the assistive technology section. In addition, there are a number of tools to assist online research and reference aids. These include: Zotero, Mandalay and Yahoo Search Pad. These facilitate saving notes, bookmarking and storing references.

Authorship of coursework

However, there is one issue of considerable importance, which is authorship of the work. There has always been a question about who has done the coursework – the person whose name is at the top, a loving parent, a helpful friend, or increasingly has it been written as part of a commercial transaction? This is not a new issue, and there are even anecdotes of well-intentioned tutors telling students what to write in an essay rather than teaching them the skills to do it for themselves. The problem is that most of this 'helping', whether it is a word of advice or intentional online collaboration designed to provide a higher grade, is almost impossible to detect.

However, there is a second dimension, which is that the writer may use the internet for reference material, and some of that material may be included, either accidentally or intentionally, in the final document. This is plagiarism, and is a major source of problems for many institutions.

Plagiarism

Plagiarism is a real problem in the digital world which may be defined as 'the unauthorized use or close imitation of the language and thoughts of another author and the representation of them as one's own original work' (www.dictionary.com). There are two types of plagiarism: the intentional and unintentional use. The former is widely discussed on the internet, and does not require further expansion here. However, given the context here is dyslexia in the digital age, we need to consider the relevant issues.

Today's knowledge-hungry world is dominated by the internet, and the way to research an essay, thesis or subject manner is usually via the internet, either through dedicated academic search engines, or through the more open access systems of Yahoo! and Google. In the past, one could read a paper version of an article, and then retype and rephrase everything. The painstaking and laborious nature of the work was a significant disincentive, but you knew exactly where you were. Today the availability of everything in electronic forms means that it is too easy to go to a page, and because you are so worried about losing the reference, you copy and paste the phrase, sentence or paragraph into your own document to save doing the search again.

The problem arises when you can no longer remember what is your text and what is somebody else's. So the passage remains in the text in its original format, thus creating 'accidental plagiarism'. This is not to suggest that dyslexics are more likely to be accidental plagiarists, but one should be aware that somebody with memory issues, with organizational problems, and who may have difficulty with re-reading what they have written could become an accidental plagiarist. The answer obviously is to avoid this method, but the reality is that it is too easy to get lost on the internet. So there are alternatives to consider, such as never paste directly into your final document or highlight in bright red (or whichever colour you prefer).

But in real life, this may not always happen. Fortunately the same open access to information that creates the problem also provides the solution. Most academic institutions will now have anti-plagiarism software installed or as a subscription service. Lecturers can submit essays to check the authorship of the material. However, the accidental plagiarizer can also check his or her works prior to submission, thereby avoiding that embarrassing meeting to explain similarities between his or her work and what appears on the web. Unfortunately there are also some cheats who will repeatedly modify and submit until they are no longer detected in the systems. However, they are few and far between. (For further information on plagiarism, try www.plagiarism.org.)

Examples of plagiarism checkers include Checkforplagiarism, Copyscape, Copytracker, Plagiarismchecker, Plagiarismdetect, Plagium, Turnitin and Writecheck.

Although technically not plagiarism, there is also the potential in the near future to routinely check for consistency of a student's work. For example, it would be possible to check the consistency between the submitted coursework and the examination answers. One would expect greater internal consistency if the two were done by the same person than if they were done by different people. Visions of what Web 3.0 can do, where there will be greater emphasis on semantic relationships in search and knowledge management, suggest that this may become routine. The question then arises, what if the consistency between coursework and examinations is less for a dyslexic individual (as one would expect due to the lack of support in exams) than for the average population?

Examinations and computers

While the examinee is the person to whom the certificate of competence applies, it is the person who is making decisions based on that certificate who needs to be reassured of the significance of that certificate. That is, they need to know three key facts:

1. that the person sitting the exam is the same one as named on the certificate;
2. that the exam was a reasonable measure of what is claimed on the certificate;
3. that any differences for reasons of disability did not offer unfair advantage or disadvantage.

The first of these (authorship) is a long-standing problem and is not new to technology. If the examination is taken on a computer, there may be issues to consider. However, technology can also come to the rescue.

Case study 13 Computer-based examination in Norway

In May 2009, in Norway, students wrote all their essays on their own computers in a central hall. At a given moment they were given online access to the examination paper, and proceeded to complete it on their own computers. Although assistive technology was not specifically mentioned in the review, the fact that they were able to use their own computers meant they could use the software they had loaded, which presumably could include text-to-speech and speech-to-text. The usually cited problem of cheating was, in effect, circumvented by installing on all computers a form of tracking software which recorded keystrokes and could detect any attempts to by-pass the blocks in place to stop students accessing the internet during the exams. This appears to signal the way forward for all, and would help overcome many of the problems dyslexic students face when having to do examinations on computers.

While it is understandable that some people would worry about what information could be accessed during an examination, it should also be remembered the problems that face a dyslexic student when faced with a new computer, though in the past few years regulators have begun to see the light. They have moved from simply providing a virgin computer with assistive technology, to at least technology that is the same. However, some of these technologies 'learn' the responses of the user, and therefore using newly installed software may be a very different experience to using trained software. One way round this is to load the 'profiles' (e.g., the profile from a speech-to-text application) from a USB memory stick prior to the exam (and then make sure it works properly!).

However, there is still the question of the use of simple study aids. If a dyslexic student normally uses reminders of how to plan an essay, are they discriminated against if they are not allowed to use them in an examination?

Computerized marking

Increasingly the computer is also being used to mark students' electronic papers. This is said to be due to lower costs, to relieve the burden of administration from teacher and lecturers and give greater consistency. However, research suggests that the human and financial savings may not be as much as the marketing suggests. Increased uptake of automated services and greater competition will drive down costs, but currently the cost of obtaining a mark for a paper using computers is similar to that using a human marker.

Clearly the main areas currently under consideration for computerized marking are:

1. multiple choice questions
2. short text answers
3. open essays
4. concept mapping.

Multiple choice questions

Multiple choice questions are the simplest to computerize since the analysis is only a matter of providing a series of alternatives, which are assessed as right or wrong. Issues for dyslexic individuals are that many have great problems when faced with a whole mass of multiple choice questions on a single page. By presenting them one at a time, this problem is relieved. Furthermore, the computer should be able to offer alternatives for the user interface, which may be important to the dyslexic user (see the box below). The dyslexic individual may also be disadvantaged if the mark is either right or wrong, which is usually the case. Many dyslexic individuals confuse similar words. However, if the alternative responses are graded, they may do considerably better than if a yes/no response is used.

Layout of multiple choice questions

The Dystrain Project survey looked at the layout of buttons on a multiple choice question. The survey included an attempt to further understand the multiple choice format that is preferred.

> Non-dyslexics preferred – Vertical with tick box before the response (85 per cent).

> Mildly and moderately dyslexics preferred – Vertical with tick box before the response (35 per cent), 50 per cent preferred horizontal (preferably with the tick before the item).

In 2007, a case in the UK press highlighted a dyslexic medical student who took her examination board to court as she claimed she failed because the multiple choice exam was presented in a format that disadvantaged her.

Short text answers

Short text answers enable a small data set of target words to be used for reference, without providing the clues that are available in multiple choice questions. The advantage to dyslexic individuals is that they do not have to write long essays. The disadvantage is that not all systems have spellcheckers, and the vocabulary used by the dyslexic examinee may be different from that residing in the reference data bank. However, there is no known research to confirm the use of this type of system and the problems faced by the dyslexic individual.

Open essays

There is little doubt that a major area for development in education in the next ten years will be automated marking of essays. Web 3.0 seems to promise greater use of semantic analysis, which will be the successor to the original work on latent semantic analysis and related techniques in the late 1990s (see, e.g., Landauer et al. 1998). The principles have been around for a number of years, and attempts to develop a theoretical map with distances between keywords being a measure of the quality of the work. There are claims that the correlation between the computer and a human marker is at least as good as (human) inter-rater correlations. However, the difficulty is in developing a sufficiently large enough database on a subject prior to marking a specific topic. Given the range of questions that could be asked, and the different levels at which they would be (e.g., from secondary school to post-graduate level), it would be difficult to imagine a usable system in the short term. However, the move towards online systems, and the storage or student responses online mean the quantity of data available for compiling comparative data sets will increase exponentially as Web 3.0 kicks in. This will make it a viable proposition in national examinations (e.g., GCSE exams) where a good quantity of exemplars are available.

But what of the impact on the dyslexic writer? Again there has been no research done in this field to suggest it will be either of benefit or to the detriment of the dyslexic individual. One view is that since it looks for keywords, and distance between them, the structure may be less important than in human-based systems. There may be advantages to the dyslexic examinee, but until the systems are specifically tried with dyslexic writers, any institutions looking to implement this system for all students may find themselves subject to some serious questions that might result in court cases citing discrimination due to the marking methodology.

Concept mapping

Most dyslexic individuals will at some point attempt to learn how to make concept maps (sometimes referred to as mind maps). Their use and development are covered elsewhere in this book as well as extensively on the internet. Here we shall concentrate on the use of electronic concept maps in examinations. As many dyslexic individuals have argued, if the concept map is said to represent the essay, why can it not be submitted as 'the essay'?

The problem is, how do you evaluate a concept map, especially when the exam process is normative – that is you are comparing with other people, most of whom have submitted traditional essays? This is a real challenge, and it is rare that a concept map could give as much information as an essay. That said, it need not be the case, and sometimes a concept map may provide more information, more accessibly than the essay. (See the accompanying website for various rubrics about concept map assessment.)

It may be argued that, in most cases, some sort of prioritization of the components is required, to suggest what information is most important and the order of presentation of the information in the linear essay is important. Although the software frequently provides a version that converts the map into a linear version, the manner in which it does this is, at best, dubious.

There has been some research in this field of concept map marking. However, the quality of the research is at best variable, it is carried out under 'laboratory' conditions, the theoretical constructs used are of variable quality and the impact of dyslexia has not been investigated. Researchers are attempting to investigate the two methods: (1) analyse the traits using predetermined criteria (for criteria references see the website); and (2) analyse the entire concept map using certain key characteristics with respect to an exemplar (norm referenced). In brief, the evaluation process looks at the semantic relationship between the nodes (the main ideas) as well as the links between them. Once an acceptable, reliable system has been developed, this will become a standard for testing procedure.

Results to date are reasonable, with the correlation between computer and human-assessed concept maps being greater than with essays. For example, Koul et al. (2005) produced computer-based evaluation of concepts map comparing them with human evaluation, and were considered to be a good measure of the qualitative aspects of the concept maps ($r = 0.84$) and were an adequate measure of the quantitative aspects ($r = 0.65$). However, it should be noted that the concept maps had been evaluated against a set of criteria, and those criteria had been used for human and computer evaluation. Thus the value is really a reflection of the computer's ability to use the same criteria, rather than necessarily being a good measure of the quality of the concept map.

There is little doubt that Web 3.0 methods, which rely more on semantic relationships, will boost the development of software that can evaluate concept maps. Furthermore, it is possible to envisage greater access to more and more concepts maps that may become part of a wider database. However, until such time as these exist, the acceptance of concept maps as an alternative to essays, their marking, and most importantly their computerized marking, will remain outside mainstream usage.

Conclusion

This chapter has not attempted to cover all aspects of e-learning and knowledge assessment because: (1) it is largely covered in other books; and (2) there is little research that has specifically been with respect to the dyslexic individual. Instead issues have been raised that should be the concern of educators and developers. Tools that are available and their potential impact have been discussed. There is little doubt that the role of e-learning and computer-based assessments will increase. And this is why there is an urgent need to develop research proposals that cover in an education-led (rather than technology-led) manner the diverse preferences and responses of the dyslexic learner.

8 Multilingualism

Introduction

This chapter is about providing support to the dyslexic individual who is attempting to deal with more than one language. The difficulties of identification and general support of the dyslexic 'multilingual' child are covered elsewhere (see, e.g., Smythe and Everatt 2002; Smythe 2004, 2005), as are those of the multilingual adult (Smythe and Capellini 2007). Therefore, this chapter will discuss the role of ICT, within a theoretical framework, and suggest it may help overcome a number of the issues. Although the main topic will be those with English as a second language, much of the material can be adapted to learning another language when English is the first language.

In this chapter, we shall look at how technology can be used to support the multilingual dyslexic individual as well as those who are learning a second language, but whose first language is English. However, before that, we need to consider what the key issues are, both in terms of cognitive skills and deficits and with respect to how technology could be used for support.

The final part of this chapter provides a brief introduction to many language- and translation-related systems that can assist the multilingual dyslexic individual.

Cognitive difficulties faced by multilingual dyslexic individuals

The cognitive loads in first language literacy learning were set out in Chapter 1, and we can use this as a way of understanding the main areas of difficulty for the dyslexic multilingual individual. These are:

- auditory processing
- phonological skills
- speech/sound synthesis
- visual processing
- orthographic processing
- motor skills
- lexical skills.

There are also a number of other skills which are important, which will be discussed later.

Much of the support that is suggested for monolingual dyslexic individuals also works for multilingual dyslexic individuals. However, as suggested above, since the multilingual individual may be less practised in the sound of the language, there are additional techniques that can be used. It is clear that blended learning, rather than technology-led learning, it the answer. Without the human component, any computer-based activity may be little more than a series of strategies to finish the activity rather than consolidating learning to use in other contexts.

Note that, while in this section the technology suggestions are set against specific cognitive difficulties, it does not mean that they will have an impact only in that area. The technology can be used to support the specific deficits discussed above.

Auditory processing

If an individual is having problems distinguishing between two sounds, it will be difficult for them to spell the word. For example, the Spanish child may have problems with 'b'/'p' (telling the difference between 'pin' and 'bin'), the Gujerati speaker often has problems with 'f'/'v' ('fan'/'van') while the Chinese and Japanese have problems with 'l'/'r' ('lip'/'rip'). Any assessment of the difficulties of the dyslexic individual should include a measure of auditory processing/sound discrimination preferably with respect to the language in question. Many teachers and testers ignore this aspect of assessment and teaching, assuming that this has been checked as part of a standard (regular) medical check-up. However, with the multilingual individual, such assumptions cannot be made. Testing in the first language of the multilingual dyslexic individual is often impractical due to the lack of testers who can use the appropriate language. However, technology can assist by providing resources that can be shared for testing in key languages. It is this technology-led approach that allows online assessment developers to address such issues. (See, e.g., Do-It Solutions at www.learnerprofiler.co.uk.)

Using technology to support auditory processing

Listening to sounds in context will help considerably, especially if the listener can also recognize the subtle differences between sounds. Listening to stories is a good start, provided the vocabulary is age-appropriate. However, there will be greater reinforcement if the person can also see the text highlighted as it is read. Many of the commercial packages noted in Chapter 4 can provide not only excellent speech with good intonation but can also highlight the text at the same time.

Due care and attention should be made to ensure the vocabulary set is appropriate. A good starting point for the early language learner is Charles Ogden's 850 Basic English words that allow the user to express 90 per cent of their ideas. Although now a little dated, it does provide a more useful guide than simply word frequency lists (http://ogden.basic-english.org/).

Note that, when learning languages, there is a need to see and hear a word more than once to ensure it is remembered and the links are made between the sounds, the written word and the meaning. There is considerable research that highlights this, and a number of resources exist to help check the appropriateness of text. (For a good review, see Cobb 2007. The related website is, www.lextutor.ca.)

Phonological skills

It is well documented, and repeated earlier in this book, that the development of phonological skills is key to the acquisition of good literacy skills. Without them, self-learning will be at best problematic. The learner may have failed to learn these skills for several reasons. For example, if rhyming skills are not important in your first language, you may not develop the level of rhyming necessary for good English literacy skills, even though you acquire adequate skills in your first language. Furthermore, just because an individual has apparently been taught English, it does not mean he or she has been taught phonics appropriately. If he or she has not had the opportunity to acquire the skills, you cannot say whether he or she has had a difficulty in the acquisition of the skills and therefore cannot say that person is dyslexic. It might be that those skills (e.g., rhyming) were not important in their first language and they were not acquired implicitly and explicitly during learning, or perhaps they were taught poorly, or perhaps the individual has difficulty acquiring such skills. Failing to teach and consolidate the foundation means anything beyond that will only have limited success.

If a child has difficulty with phonological skills, then that is what needs to be taught, irrespective of the first language. The difference will be that the monolingual dyslexic individual may know the words, while the multilingual dyslexic may not. Therefore the learning may be more laboured since he or she is struggling to contextualize, e.g., the rhyming activity. Currently there is no software aimed at teaching phonological skills to this user group. Therefore due care and attention should be taken when selecting software, in particular with respect to contextual vocabulary. That is, the child may know 'cat, hat and mat', but does not know the words in capitals in the associated sentence 'Can you HEAR that the ENDS of these words SOUND the SAME?'

Speech/sound synthesis

As we learn to speak, we are learning how to put all the different parts together to make the appropriate sound. Feedback is usually in the form of somebody telling us it is right or wrong, and how to correct it. When learning a second language, we still need this practice, to create the engrams (the patterns) in our motor memory that mean we can repeat the sound easily. Dyslexic individuals learning a second language may have problems due to the difficulty of recalling the exact sound so they can try to repeat it, or can be confused between similar sounds and may have difficulty in controlling the parts of the mouth to make those sounds.

As with the other activities related to the multilingual dyslexic individual, there is little that can replace the informed teacher and/or parent. However, some have found that software that provides a visual representation of sounds can help provide feedback and correct errors. This helps convince those children who say 'It sounds right to me'. This may be in the form of standard sound recording software (e.g., the freeware Audacity) or specialist software such as Chatback (available from Xavier Educational Software). As with other activities, the support person must also have a firm grasp of the language being taught, including correct pronunciation.

Visual processing

The problems with visual processing for multilingual dyslexic individuals are similar to those of monolingual dyslexic individuals. The specific needs will depend on the level and nature of the problem. However, the issues of visual processing are different from those of orthographic processing, and are principally the concern of the optician. Some software does exist, such as those activities to be found in Edysgate (www.edysgate. com). These are about recognizing shapes within backgrounds, and visual memory, and can provide some basic support with concern for the first language or the level of literacy.

Orthographic processing

Orthographic processing can cover everything from the recognition of a single letter (especially if they use a script very different from English, such as Arabic or Chinese), to whole word recognition. In the middle are letter clusters, which may be used to form a single sound (e.g., 'sh' in 'ship'), or be combined to make a sound that does not conform to a letter-by-letter construction (e.g., '-ight' in words like 'light' and 'night'). The orthographic processing also allows us to identify 'illegal' letter combinations when spelling (e.g., '-fv' is not a letter combination at the end of an English word).

It is well known that children learn that they need to identify finer detail to distinguish between words and eventually letters as they learn literacy skills. In the same way, if the child is young, or is very new to the language, he or she may need assistance at the simple letter level, to distinguish between, say, 'c', 'e' and 'o', or the ones commonly known to cause a problem for dyslexic individuals, such as 'b' and 'd'. Simple computer-based activities of the 'embedded figures' (e.g., picture within a picture) type work well, and can even be made in software such as PowerPoint.

Motor skills

Motor skills are required for handwriting and typing. If the individual has not been introduced to proper letter formation using pen and paper, he or she will have difficulty developing legible handwriting.

Although there are some software programs that can analyse handwriting using independent tablets or tablet PCs, these are still research tools and are not widely available.

However, with the increased use of computers, which are a boon to multilingual learners, it would seem logical to teach typing skills through appropriate interactive typing tutors, preferably using phonics (see Chapter 5). Unfortunately, most available packages are designed for the monolingual individual, and would be taxing on the individual with restricted vocabulary. Although, it is possible to use a number of freeware packages where you set your own typing lists.

Lexical skills

Increasing vocabulary is an important step in the learning procedure for dyslexic multilingual individuals. Too many teachers try to help by focusing on the written word. However, it is the combination of spoken and written words, clearly linked to the meaning, that is the key to success. Simple vocabulary used in appropriate contexts (e.g., using role play to order pizza with extra toppings) is important, but better performed between individuals than with a computer, not least because the teacher can evaluate relative skills quicker than the computer.

The best way to use technology to assist development of lexical skills is to read e-books, listen to podcasts and use text-to-speech software that highlights the words as they are read. This will provide a good pronunciation guide and clearly map the words to the sounds. As the vocabulary increases, so the need to provide this at all times decreases. An intermediate version is, for example, to use the sound on a needs basis rather than with every word. This could be for copy and paste or as a look-up system.

There are several look-up versions, including Answertips (www.answers. com) which has both sounds and translations. However, this relies on certain codes being embedded on the website. Other online versions that may be used in certain circumstances include Google (www.google.com/ language_tools?hl=en) and Babylon (www.babylon.com). Some (e.g., http:// imtranslator.com) provide not only the ability to speak the text, but also translate from one language to another and back again to check the quality of the translation.

Offline versions which reside on your computer can be more flexible since they do not require the internet connection.

Types of multilingualism

The issues of learning a language other than the mother tongue arise in a number of contexts. The following examples assume the learner is dyslexic.

1. *English children learning a second language.* As second language learning is a curriculum requirement (especially in countries where a baccalaureate system is in place), most learners do not have the choice in many circumstances. But if the child is already so far behind in a subject that he or she will have little chance of success, then the technology will be of little use. However, motivation may be an important part, and if the technology (through projects such as Calldysc – see p. 146) can help, it would be better to personalize the work at a much lower level.

2. *Bilingual children resident in England, with English as a second language.* In the UK, the most common multilingual context will be the child who has grown up in an English language learning environment, but with parents (and possibly friends, neighbours and the community) who speak a language other than English. In many cases, the child may have been born elsewhere, and may even have been taught English abroad. However, no assumptions should be made about the quality of that English teaching, especially with respect to learning phonics. Vocabulary may be less than age-appropriate, and he or she may have trouble hearing some of the sounds.

3. *Bilingual children 'visiting' the UK.* The reason for the 'visit' may be due to parents working in the country on a temporary contract, or the child could be at boarding school. Either way, they are normally coming into an English immersion context, but have not had long-term exposure to the language, and may have also learned another script. Often inappropriate assumptions are made about prior phonics learning.

4. *Multilingual children in a multilingual environment.* Some children are taught in international schools, where the language of tuition is English, but the children are from many language backgrounds. This will have an impact on their pronunciation, as they can only try to copy the sounds others make.

Bilingualism in Wales

Wales is a special case since it is a bilingual country, with primary and secondary schools where children are taught the curriculum through the medium of Welsh. Furthermore, it is becoming increasingly difficult to find jobs in politics or the media unless you are fluent in Welsh.

What is surprising is that there is still a shortage of Welsh medium resources, particularly for the dyslexic individual (see p. 179). Therefore, it. is possible that a child is brought up in the medium of English and then goes to a Welsh medium school, or is brought up in Welsh and sent to an English medium school. (This may be because the first language choice is not available in the area.) Furthermore, the language spoken at home may not necessarily be the language of tuition. Consequently some children will start at a Welsh medium school not knowing any Welsh language while others will have excellent grammar and vocabulary.

This situation is exacerbated when the parents are not fluent in the language of tuition. Furthermore, due to the hereditary nature of dyslexia, many parents may also be dyslexic, and struggling to learn Welsh. Thus support with homework may also be an issue.

Motivation, technology and second language learning

A number of research projects have attempted to use the technology specifically to teach the dyslexic multilingual individual knowing that motivation to learn a new language is low. Years of failure in the first language do not encourage new language learning, especially when you realize the amount that has to be learned in terms of vocabulary, sounds and spelling. And if you cannot see a use for it, why learn?

Calldysc (Collaborative Language Learning for Dyslexic Children – see website) proved that by supplying mobile phones to dyslexic pupils to learn English in places as diverse as Poland, Hungary and Bulgaria, the children would be engaged in language learning activities at a level far greater than they would normally be involved in when in the conventional classroom environment.

In this case, the technology provides a status symbol which can be seen by the rest of the class. But the computer (e.g., a netbook) can also be a motivator if it can provide positive feedback, and any errors are hidden from the rest of the class. That is, the technology itself can lead to the learning potential, and should be explored with the reluctant language learner.

Using assistive software to support literacy

There are two possible ways to review the match between technology and the needs of the individual learning an additional language. The conventional way is to see what the technology is and then use it to solve the problems. Or the more logical way which is to identify the problems and then see which technology exists to help. We shall use the latter approach first, and then look at that technology that can help.

Word is spoken in first language – now translate

The problems here are: (1) remembering the word or phrase; (2) translating it into the target language; and (3) pronouncing it if necessary.

If the words constitute a long phrase or passage, it is best to use some form of sound recorder so the text can be translated piece by piece. If the words are already known, it would be possible to translate them, and maybe write them down. If the translation is not known, then it may be possible to transcribe the words and then use a dictionary (paper, hand-held electronic, computer-based or online). However, this relies on the words being correctly spelled (with the aid of a spellchecker). There are a number of options for this, each of which would lead to success. The one important part, which is true for all translations, is to check the quality by translating it back into the first language. If the translations have the same meaning, it can be called a good translation.

Word is written in first language – now translate

This is an easier option since there is no need now to spell the word in the first language. However, remember that for dyslexic people, just because it is in their first language does not mean they know how to pronounce it. And usually, unless you can pronounce it, you will not know what it means. Therefore the problems can be broken down into: (1) to be able to pronounce the word; (2) to be able to translate it into the target language; and (3) to be able to pronounce the translation if necessary. All these can be resolved using multilingual text-to-speech and translation services such as www.imtranslator.com.

Word is spoken in English

This is the most problematic context for those with English as a second language. Again, the recorder is very important, so that it can be played repeatedly. If the words are not known, some attempt has to be made to write them down, and checked in a dictionary that can work with the user's spelling, no matter how bad. Several online services suggest they can find the target word no matter how wrong, provide there is a reasonable phonic representation. Once the correct word has been identified, a simple translating dictionary will suffice.

Word is written in English

If the word, phrase or paragraph is in electronic format, it can easily be translated through using pop-up translators, online dictionaries or translation services. These can then speak the text if required.

Whose words are they?

Think about this – if an English child is set some French homework, e.g. to write a brief story about his or her holiday, and he or she writes it in English and then uses an online translation service to get an instant translation, can you say he or she has done his or her homework?

This is a very real issue for the teacher today. Of course, the problem was always there, since formerly a parent or sibling could have done the homework and not the child. But now, with such sophisticated online services, nobody except the perpetrator will know.

In the UK, there is no baccalaureate system, and given that many dyslexic individuals will opt out of taking a language examination, it may be no loss if they use such a system. If anything it will be a gain since it lowers their stress. Of course, it does not help them learn the language. But then many would feel that is no loss.

Using language in the age of technology: the Emime project

The Emime project, a collaboration led by the University of Edinburgh, Nokia and others, aims to take the words of the speaker, translate them and then use the user's own voice to speak back the words, all on a mobile phone. If this does work as it claims to (and should be ready before 2011), then why should any dyslexic individual bother to learn a foreign language? (www.emime.org)

Assistive technology and multilingualism

Looking at the issues from a technology perspective, there are a number of software solutions which can be of benefit to the multilingual dyslexic learner. The key ones are:

- text-to-speech
- speech-to-text
- concept mapping
- spellcheckers and grammar checkers
- typing skills.

Note that these are discussed at length in Chapter 4.

Text-to-speech

For those learning English, one major advantage they have over other language learners is the large number of free and low cost text-to-speech software that is available. However, some users also need them in other languages. Although things improve regularly, three worthy of highlighting are:

- The free text-to-speech software Readplease (www.readplease.com), which is available in at least Dutch, French, German, Italian, Portuguese and Spanish.
- The free online text-to-speech website ImTranslator (http://imtranslator.com). It offers English, Chinese, French, German, Italian, Japanese, Korean, Portuguese, Russian and Spanish, complete with a talking avatar.
- The commercial software ClaroRead can work with Australian English, Belgian, Brazilian, British English, Cantonese, Czech, Danish, Dutch, French, French-Canadian, German, Greek, Indian English, Italian, Japanese, Korean, Mandarin, Mexican, Norwegian, Polish, Portuguese, Russian, Spanish, Swedish, Taiwanese, Turkish and USA English.

Speech-to-text and speech analysis

To be useful to the multilingual speaker, the user may need to be both creative and patient to use speech-to-text. For example, although the software comes with a fixed vocabulary and the accents are limited, significant retraining can be achieved. This means a heavy Welsh accent can use standard 'English' voices, and adjust it. However, the training period may increase considerably. This means the Chinese or Gujerati speaker with a strong accent could also use it. DragonDictate (from Nuance) is also available in Dutch, French, German, Italian and Spanish, opening the way for practising these languages. The latest version (version 10) is now so sophisticated that little training is required. While this may entail more for dyslexic multilingual students, it is well worth trying.

Concept mapping

If the lack of language skills (e.g., spoken vocabulary) is impairing progress and hindering engaging in the school activities (e.g., writing a short story in French for an English first language person, or writing in English for those with English as a second language), concept mapping tools are an alternative for presentation. Clearly if the first language of the user or the language of tuition is English, then drop-down menus in other languages may not be important. But in some cases (e.g., MindFull), they can be changed. Free tools such as ikonmaps (www.ikonmap.com) are designed with few words, and are available in many languages, including English, Spanish, French, Italian, Dutch, German, Russian and Chinese.

Spellcheckers and grammar checkers

As with monolingual individuals, spelling and grammar checkers are very important for the second language learner. There are many options from those built into word processors such as Microsoft Word and Open Office to those available on the mobile phone.

Typing skills

In the UK now, many children grow up in a computer learning environment, and acquire typing skills. However, many multilingual children may not have these skills, although they may acquire them the same way that any dyslexic individual would, through the use of a good typing tutor. There are many typing tutors to choose from, but probably the best would be one where you can choose which words to use for practice.

Furthermore, those children who have a script that is very different from the English script (e.g., Chinese or Arabic) may also find the transition to a new script difficult. Using keyboards may help make it easier.

Mobile phone language learning

The advantage of the ubiquitous mobile phone has led to widespread research into its use as a learning platform, including with respect to those with cognitive difficulties (see, e.g., Chen et al. 2008). A number of projects have involved English language learning, of which Calldysc is the only one dedicated to helping the dyslexic individual (see website). However, this is not a full course, and was designed to show that motivation improves the potential to learn and what developers could achieve.

Mobile phones can be very useful as ancillary tools, however, most importantly they can provide a look-up dictionary that could be a translating dictionary as well as a spellchecker and definitions dictionary. Furthermore, as well as being used locally like this, the mobile can be used as an internet browser for certain activities, such as checking grammar and punctuation issues. It may also provide a bridge to the first language.

Using technology for translation

There has been a rapid increase in the number of machine translation software available in the past few years. No longer are we restricted to the desktop offline translation in common language using cut and paste. And the quality has also greatly improved. Below are a number of different types that have their advantages, many of which will be very useful to the dyslexic user depending on the context. Some systems are integral – that is they have a translation (and back translation necessary for checking the quality of the translation) as well as the ability to speak it out loud. Others could be used in combination with additional services, such as those listed on the text-to-speech in Chapter 4.

Browser translators

The Mozilla Firefox development community has produced many extensions for diverse languages that may be of interest. The most popular ones are:

- gTranslate
- BabelFish Instant Translation
- bab.la dictionary toolbar
- FoxLingo,

Desktop translation widgets

A number of translation widgets are available that actively use other translation services such as Google. Examples of sources include:

- Yahoo Widgets (for desktop applications)
- Google Gadgets (for integration into iGoogle).

Built-in web page translation

Several tools can be built into a web page for instant translation. The two listed here are both used for the TechnoDys website:

- Google Translate
- Babelfish.

Free online translators

In these websites, you can usually type in or copy and paste text, or have a specific web page translated:

- Imtranslator – includes text-to-speech and a talking avatar
- Freetranslation
- Online-translator
- Google Translate.

An example of a 'mash-up' can be found at http://translate.1888usa. com/. On this page, on one side you type your text into a Google translator, and then copy paste it into the other side where it is spoken using AT&T technology. There are few voices available currently. However, this type of combination will probably be more common in the future, although with the transfer between technologies being done automatically.

Welsh language resources

Although there is a distinct lack of Welsh language resources, a number should be mentioned:

- Welsh Talking Word Processor – Edgair. The product is available through the Welsh Dyslexia Project website www.welshdyslexia.info.
- Claro Scan2Text. Claro Scan2Text can convert paper, pdfs and images to editable and readable text in standard word processors including in the Welsh language.
- Open Office. A Welsh version of this free office software is available for download from www.meddal.com/.
- Terminology dictionary for mobiles. It is possible to download for free a Welsh-English 'Terminology Dictionary' for your mobile phone at http://geiriadur:bangor.ac.uk/termiadur/ffon_en.html.
- Microsoft Office 2007. There is a Welsh spellchecker now available for Office 2007.
- BBC Welsh language games. Those trying to understand the Welsh spelling could try www.bbc.co.uk/cymru/raw/gemau/rygbi/index.shtml. However, good spoken Welsh is required.
- Cysgliad. This contains Cysill (a Welsh grammar and spellchecker) and Cysgeir, a suite of Welsh/English dictionaries in electronic format: www.e-gymraeg.org/cysgliad/.
- Clicker. This is advertised as providing the ability to create your own talking books: www.cricksoft.com/uk/ideas/using_clicker/talking_books_reading3.htm.

Further resources can be found at:

- Welsh Dyslexia Project – www.welshdyslexia.info
- BBC – www.bbc.co.uk/wales/learnwelsh/links/index.shtml
- Canolfan Bedwyr – www.bangor.ac.uk/ar/cb/meddalwedd.php.

Hovering

A number of free and commercial software systems enable you to hover over a word and either hold down a designated key or click twice. Examples include:

- ClaroLingo
- Answertips.

Handheld hardware

There are a number of handheld devices that can be used to scan the text to provide a translation. Examples include:

- Quicktionary
- InfoScan
- ReadingPen + Portable scanning translator.

Translation tools on a mobile

There are an increasing number of translation tools that are designed for the mobile phone, particular for text used in communications such as email, SMS and instant messaging. An internet search will produce many mobile dictionaries:

- Transclick.com – Mobile translation of SMS, email and Instant Messaging
- Moka – Translation of Skype and text messages (currently only English, Chinese and Spanish).

Speech-to-speech translators

There are a few devices where you can speak into the microphone and it speaks back the translation:

- Ectaco – handheld device using fixed voices
- Emime – under development at Edinburgh University. It will speak back using your own voice. Scheduled availability 2011.

Commercial translation software

Many examples of software are available, and these change on a regular basis. For a comparison of translation software see http://translation-software-review.toptenreviews.com/. Beware: not all have built in text-to-speech software.

Lists of translation tools

There are many websites dedicated to supplying lists of translation tools. Here is one that appears to be regularly updated: www.omniglot.com/links/translation.htm.

Online resources

The problem with recommending website and resources is that they change so quickly. Hence, for most chapters, the reader is referred to a website for the latest information. However, there are several websites that can help the additional language learner, each of which has been in existence for at least five years. The first two are resources which also have links to other resources, while the BBC has developed its own resources.

However, it is important to remember that these are not designed to support the dyslexic individual, and therefore you will find little emphasis on some of the underlying skills known to be important. These may be there implicitly, but not explicitly. However, by understanding the principles as set out in this chapter, it should be possible to use such resources. A link is also provided to a relevant online e-journal. Do not forget to also check the dedicated website for more links.

1. Languages and ICT. This website has been developed by the National Centre for Languages (CILT) with the Association for Language Learning (ALL): www.languages-ict.org.uk/.
2. Information and communication technology for language teachers. This is a privately run website based on an EU project website, with links to many resources, including website and professional organizations: www.ict4lt.org/.
3. BBC Learning English. A collection of resources and ideas for all those teaching and learning English: www.bbc.co.uk/worldservice/learningenglish/.
4. *Language Learning and Technology Journal.* A refereed journal for second and foreign language educators: http://llt.msu.edu/.
5. Dyslexia and foreign language learning. This is a private site maintained by Dr Margaret Crombie, a specialist in the field of dyslexia and the teaching of foreign languages: www.hilarymccoll.co.uk/dyslexia.html.
6. TechnoDys. A blog dedicated to dyslexia and technology which includes many resources that can be used with the multilingual learner: http://technodys.blogspot.com/.
7. Integrating ICT into the MFL classroom. In this blog, Joe Dale offers many general (i.e. not dyslexia-specific) practical tips and advice on using ICT to enhance the teaching of modern foreign languages: http://joedale.typepad.com/

Conclusion

There are many difficulties that the multilingual dyslexic individual has to overcome, including the misapprehension that they cannot be helped. But, as this chapter shows, this need not be the case. As with the dyslexic monolingual individual, first, you need to identify the issues, and then set about supporting the areas of weakness. The biggest danger that the dyslexic individual faces is the assumptions of those who are supposed to offer support.

In the end, the label is irrelevant, unless it is to provide additional funding. If individuals have a specific problem, then they need support in that area, irrespective of any label. The support detailed in this chapter was with respect to the needs of the individual, targeting support to needs, and it will improve in future. However, clearly there is a lot out there already.

Arguably the area that is still most in need of attention is the assessment process. But, once more, if a social model is envisioned for the future, then services should be provided for everyone without the need to prove to a given label. To be able to assess in a thousand different first languages would be some achievement, but it would totally miss the point. What is needed is the implementation of appropriate support, and in most cases that is in the language of tuition or the workplace.

9

Conclusion: Spreading the Word

Introduction

This book is about technology, and the speed of change of technology is considerable. Everything is changing rapidly, and that change, more than any government legislation, is what is going to make the provision more widespread.

Rapidly falling costs of computers and laptops make their use very much mainstream. This drives down the cost of assessment and support. With online assessment having been a reality for several years, there are now signs of mainstream uptake, which will revolutionize the assessment process. It may not be so far away when not only can the dyslexic individual have easy access to online assessment, but those assessments could become mainstream activities for everybody.

Following that, the dyslexic individual already has access to many forms of assistive software, and with each successive version of Operating System bringing even more free benefits, it is easy to imagine that all the necessary software will be available free soon anyway.

In trying to draw together the issues around what needs to happen in future, what can happen and what will happen, I have drawn up a ten-point plan for the future. This is based on an earlier model developed in response to an EU call for suggestions for what legislation was needed for the implementation of accessibility guidelines. My submission suggested that it was not guidelines that were needed, but the following would be more productive.

Ten-point plan for the future

1. *Engage the designers in the process.* One of the biggest problems is that the ubiquitous availability of the computer makes everybody think they can be a website designer with the aid of a little software. Conversely, the failure to show good designers how they can use their creativity to implement accessibility (it should be designer-led and not technologist-led) has encouraged designers to ignore the accessibility issues as they see them as stifling their creativity. There should be greater engagement of the creative developers, and those who teach them. See also point 6. Feedback from all the users – dyslexic individuals, tutors, assessors, support groups, employers, universities – is important.

2. *Engage the software developers.* There is no reason why the developers of the software, including browser developers (e.g., Microsoft Internet Explorer, Mozilla, Firefox, Safari and Google Chrome) as well as principal website design software developers (e.g., Adobe DreamWeaver) could not be engaged to ensure all accessibility issues are adequately covered. For example, zooming can be implemented with a simple click and there is no reason why background changes cannot be done as simply. There are a number of problems with text-to-speech engines, such as the need to use full stops at the end of headers and difficulties with lists. However, it need not be like that. HTML coding has components that the software could recognize to allow it to treat text accordingly.

3. *The EU needs to ensure its own sites are compliant with dyslexia guidelines.* The page entitled Focus eAccessibility (http://ec.europa.eu/information_society/policy/accessibility/index_en.htm) is not a good example for designers. The page is too cluttered, and does not have any buttons for accessibility. If you use the menus, you can change background colours, but the clarity of navigation decreases. The EU and other recognized bodies, such as government departments and the WAI, should practise what they preach.

4. *Create guidelines that are easy for everyone to interpret.* There are WAI guidelines, but they are not easy to follow for designers and those interested in implementation. They need to be made simpler (more accessible) for the end user. Their page on changing background colour offers out-of-date information. The design of the WAI website suggests a lack of engagement with the design community.

5. *Create good exemplars*. Good exemplars need to be created for others to follow, as currently these do not exist. These should include examples such as the Cabinet Office, the Equality and Human Rights Commission (EHRC) and the British Dyslexia Association (e.g., the EHRC site allows you to change the colour, but only affects the main background colour, and does not change the colour of the main body text area. The BDA site has templates, but that menu can hide the result of a Find). If there were good exemplars, then they would become the standards that everyone followed.

6. *Engage the user group*. It is always important to engage the user group. However, due care and attention needs to be paid with respect to the dyslexic individual since while the needs of the deaf and blind community are well defined, every dyslexic is different, and many do not know what is possible. Furthermore, the organizations that represent these groups rarely have the appropriate expertise to comment. Every opportunity should be given for this group to provide input, through a combination of open calls for comments and directed invitations. In our modern society, feedback is important as the technology is changing rapidly and feedback can influence the direction the latest technology will follow.

7. *Create a publicity campaign*. There is a lack of understanding of the issues facing dyslexic individuals, and the solutions, both within the user group and society in general. For example, few people know about zooming in browsers using Ctrl + +/-. The government should raise the awareness of the difficulties of living with dyslexia. The impact of a 30-second public information film would benefit huge numbers of people.

8. *Set out a five-year plan for compliance with existing legislation.* In theory, it is already possible to bring a lawsuit again a website if it fails to be accessible, since it contravenes the Disability Discrimination Act. The government should promote good accessibility and its advantages, but also warn of the consequences of failing to comply. Raise awareness of the legal implications of discrimination.

9. *Make the dyslexia Quality Mark part of government procurement processes*. Fulfil the guidelines of the EU aims to award tenders only to those who can demonstrate their compliance with dyslexia Quality Marks.

10. *Adopt the social model and give appropriate technology to all*. Instead of giving provision to only those few individuals who have been identified as having problems, provide the appropriate technology to everybody.

In conclusion

Hindsight provides us with the ability to show how wrong we can be. Predicting the future especially in the field of technology is, at best, problematic. Wasn't it an executive in IBM who in 1970s predicted that nobody would need more than one megabyte of memory on their machine? Clearly he has been proved wrong. And yet today, as data management goes from offline to online, he is not as wrong as he was five years ago.

There is little doubt that hardware will continue to get faster and smaller. Yet fundamentally it will still be doing the same thing. What we need to do is stand back and say, what do we need it to do? What are the difficulties that we are trying to overcome? And could these ideas also help others?

Yes, increasing processing power will allow speech-to-text to be faster and more accurate. But if we did not have the faster hardware, then we would probably find more efficient algorithms, use more parallel processing methods and use context as a greater clue than we currently do.

What will change, will be the portability of devices. We can expect to see roll-up screens and projector mobile phones becoming more common in the near future. Scanning using mobile phones, with text-to-speech, will no longer be a novelty. But my guess is that we shall end up with two devices: one designed as the primary tool, with no compromises on screen, keyboard size, data access, etc. while the second is designed for portability, and comes with compromises on ease of use and functionality. And of course the two will auto-sync.

Software is already moving rapidly from stand-alone to online. But there are already moves to produce the more robust version by combining online and offline working, ensuring no problems with data transfer speeds. Pre-processing of data, plus back-up and storage, is a logical move, while online synchronization and software updating cut costs and are more efficient.

There will also be commercial software for the specialist, but much of that used by the dyslexic individual is available free, and with successive versions of Windows and Apple OS, so more is built into the system (see, e.g., the voice recognition in Windows 7). What has changed in recent years is the greater role of advertising in free software, particularly from Google Ads. This ensures sustainability, but the distraction, especially for the dyslexic individual, can be off-putting. But then you get what you pay for.

Somewhere in between the free and commercial software is the specially commissioned software. As funding resources are increasingly squeezed, short-term gains are becoming hard to find. However, a longer view could have many benefits. Take, for example, concept mapping. Costs per person could be lowered by networking software across the institution rather than on individual machines. If a university provides commercial concept mapping across the campus via the network, plus the 'offline' version for students' stand-alone devices, there could be considerable savings.

Taking this one step further, consider how many pupils, students and employees per year are allocated this software at the expense of the taxpayer. Now consider how much it would take to make one piece of software and then give it away to everybody. This would be a perfect example of the social model of inclusion. Currently administrators are making short-term cuts. However, substantial investment such as this could not only provide major benefits to all dyslexic individuals, including those not formally diagnosed, but also produce substantial long-term financial savings.

Talking of formal assessments, there will always be a need for human assessors, particularly for those more complex cases. However, much of their work will be done in future by online services which may not have all the answers, but will at least be able to identify the key areas of difficulty and make teaching suggestions. Since the advantages of these systems will always be available (no geographical restrictions, no time restrictions, etc.), the potential for ongoing monitoring and evaluation, not just for dyslexic individuals but for everybody, is enormous, and arguably all dyslexic individuals will be identified. In future, this is more likely to be a recognition of needs rather then the provision of a label.

As technology improves (or put another way, as we become wiser in the development of the algorithms necessary to know what to teach next to the child), so the learning will become more individualized. But this can only come as the measurable benefits are seen. And the reality is that this is more likely to be through financial benefits than learning outcomes.

Of course, there is also the second director of change – the legal imperative. However, much of the legislation to ensure appropriate provision has been in place for many years. It is just not being implemented in general. People (i.e. HE administrators or HR personnel) are reluctant to make changes to the system as they see it is more hassle for them (more paperwork, arguing for more money from budgets, etc.) rather than seeing the benefits to the dyslexic individual. Legal challenges have the power to change this, and cases in the US in other disabilities are showing the potential to challenge existing systems, from institutions failing to provide comparable learning opportunities to all students to the US-based Authors' Guild who blocked text-to-speech on many of Amazon's Kindle e-books.

Fundamentally education will not change, but the details will change. The technology is not just another way of delivering education, it has the power to make it more effective, and enable (and encourage) dyslexic individuals to learn where otherwise they would fail. There has been a paradigm shift, from retaining knowledge to knowing where to find knowledge. This greatly benefits the dyslexic individual since, with poor memory, knowledge retention is problematic for them, and therefore they are more inclined to find creative ways to learn appropriate information.

So, in summary, schools will be able to use online screening and assessment tools to identify the needs of each child. In the long term, this evaluation will become integral to the learning process and not be a separate item. That assessment process will identify at an early stage which literacy skills need to be taught, and the relevant software will provide the learning, moderated through a learning management system which integrates ongoing evaluation of learning. At the same time, assistive technology will be provided. Or to be more precise, it would be suggested along with appropriate training, both of which would be pre-loaded onto the computers. That support would be available not only for dyslexic pupils in schools, but also for students, employees – in fact, all dyslexics.

And, finally, the punchline – this glimpse of the future is with us now. Much of the software is available free. Hardware prices are tumbling. Arguably all that is missing is the knowledge that the solutions are out there and the willingness to implement them.

At the end of an international dyslexia conference, I presented the following fictitious dialogue between two characters in Star Trek, Data, a human-like robot and Captain Jean Luc Picard.

> *Data*: Captain, I have encountered the word 'dyslexia' but I cannot find it in my memory. Can you explain the word, please?
> *Captain Picard*: Yes, Data. It was a term used in the late twentieth and early twenty-first centuries before we learned how to identify and support all children with problems in how to learn to read and write.

(Technical note: have you ever noticed how in science fiction films all console work is about visual interpretation and not reading words?)

The original paper was presented in 1997. If I were to rewrite it today, this would be my new version:

> *Data*: Captain, I have encountered the word 'dyslexia' but I cannot find it in my memory. Can you explain the word, please?
>
> *Captain Picard*: Yes, Data. It was a term used in the late twentieth and early twenty-first centuries before we learned how to identify and support all children with problems in how to learn to read and write. But now these children, who were failing in their schools, are now the stars of Starfleet Academy.

Technology is not the entire solution. But it can go along way towards supplying the support necessary for the dyslexic individual.

References

Agnew, J. A., Dorn, C. and Eden, G. F. (2004) 'Effect of intensive training on auditory processing and reading skills', *Brain and Language*, 88 (1), 21–5.

Alloway, T. P., Gathercole, S. E. and Pickering, S. J. (2006) 'Verbal and visuo–spatial short-term and working memory in children: are they separable?', *Child Development*, 77, 1698–716.

Alloway, T. P., Gathercole, S. E., Willis, C. S. and Adams, A.-M. (2004) 'A structural analysis of working memory and related cognitive skills in young children', *Journal of Experimental Child Psychology*, 87, 85–170.

Alty, J. L. and Beacham, N. (2006) 'An investigation into the effects that digital media can have on the learning outcomes of individuals who have dyslexia', Middlesex University Interaction Design Centre Technical Report: IDC-TR-2006–03, April.

Ashton, J., Bland, J. and Rodgers, B. (2001a) 'Impact of multimedia on motivation and concept attainment', available at: www.tcet.unt.edu/pubs/mul/mul04.pdf

Aspinall (1999) An examination of computer memory training in children', available at: www.masteringmemory.co.uk/content.asp?page=E06A5F4A-E3CB-4EF3-9C30-307E0C1C3F48

Baker, J. R. (2003) 'The Impact of paging vs. scrolling on reading online text passages', *Usability News*, 5 (1), available at: www.surl.org/usabilitynews/51/paging_scrolling.asp

Beck, J. E., Jia, P. and Mostow, J. (2003) 'Assessing student proficiency in a reading tutor that listens', *User Modeling*, 2702, 323–7.

— (2004) 'Automatically assessing oral reading fluency in a computer tutor that listens', *Technology, Instruction, Cognition and Learning*, 1, 61–81.

Bernard, M., Liao, C. and Mills, M. (2001a) 'Determining the best online font for older adults', (January), available at: www.surl.org/usabilitynews/31/fontSR.asp

Bernard, M., Mills, M., Frank, T. and McKown, J. (2001b) 'Which fonts do children prefer to read online?', (January), available at: www.surl.org/usabilitynews/31/fontJR.asp

Bernard, M., Mills, M., Peterson, M. and Storrer, K. (2001c) 'A comparison of popular online fonts: which is best and when?', (July), available at: www.surl.org/usabilitynews/32/font.asp.,

Blok, H., Oostdam, R., Otter, M. E., and Overmaat, M. (2002) 'Computer-assisted instruction in support of beginning reading instruction: a review', *Review of Education Research*, 72, 101–30.

British Psychological Society (1999) 'Guidelines for the development and use of computer-based assessments', available at: www.psychtesting.org.uk/downloadfile.cfm?file_uuid=64877B7B-CF1C-D577-971D-425278FA08CC&ext=pdf.,

Chaparro, B., Baker, J. R., Shaikh, A. D., Hull, S. and Brady, L. (2004) 'Reading online text: a comparison of four white space layouts', *Usability News*, v. 6.2, available at: http://psychology.wichita.edu/surl/usabilitynews/62/whitespace.asp.,

Chen, N. S., Hsieh, S. W. and Kinshuk (2008) 'Fitness study on short-term memory abilities and content representation types in a mobile language learning environment', *Language Learning and Technology*, 12 (3), 93–113.

Cobb, T. (2007) 'Computing the vocabulary demands of L2 reading', *Language Learning & Technology*, 32 (3), 38–63, available at: http://llt.msu.edu/vol11num3/cobb/

Draffan, E. A. and James, A. (2006) Presentation to EU Project Dystrain, May 2006.

Dyson, M. C. and Kipping, G. J. (1998) 'The effects of line length and method of movement on patterns of reading from screen', *Visible Language*, 32, 150–81.

Ecalle, J., Magnan, A., Bouchafa, H. and Gombert, J. E. (2009) 'Computer-based training with ortho-phonological units in dyslexic children: new investigations', *Dyslexia*, 15 (3), 218–38.

Elkind, J. (1998) *A Study of the Efficacy of the Kurzweil 3000 Reading Machine in Enhancing Poor Reading Performance*. Portola Valley, CA: Lexia Institute.

Gill, E. (1931) *An Essay on Typography*. London: Lund Humphries.

Gyarmathy, E. (2006) Presentation of words and sounds for mobile learning. Presentation to Calldysc Project Workshop, November.

Györfi, A. and Smythe, I. (2009) Re-engaging the SEN child into learning through social networking: a case study, online at: www.socialscience.t-mobile.hu/dok/13_Gyorfi-Smythe.pdf

Hecker, L., Burns, L., Elkind, J., Elkind, K. and Katz, L. (2002) 'Benefits of assistive reading software for students with attention disorders', *Annals of Dyslexia*, 52 (2), 243–73.

Higgins, E. L. and Raskind, M. H. (2000) 'Speaking to read: the effects of continuous vs. discrete speech recognition systems on the reading and spelling of children with learning disabilities', *Journal of Special Education Technology,* 15 (1), 19–30.

Hintikka, S., Aro, M. and Lyytinen, H. (2005) 'Computerised training of the correspondence between phonological and orphographic units', *Written Language and Literacy,* 8 (2), 155–78.

Hook, P., Macaruso, P. and Jones, S. (2001) 'Efficacy of Fast ForWord training on facilitating acquisition of reading skills by children with reading difficulties? A longitudinal study', *Annals of Dyslexia,* 51, 75–96.

Hornsby, B. and Shear, F. (1975) *Alpha to Omega*. London: Heinemann.

International Dyslexia Association (2002) available at: http://www.interdys.org/FAQWhatIs.htm

Irausquin, R. S., Drent, J. and Verhoeven, L. (2005) 'Benefits of computer-presented speed training for poor readers', *Annals of Dyslexia*, 55, 246–65.

Jiménez, J. E., Hernández-Valle, I., Ramírez, G., Ortiz, M. R., Rodrigo, M., Estevez, A., O'Shanahan, I., Garcia, E. and de la Luz Tabaue, M. (2007), 'Computer speech-based rememdiation for reading disabilities: the size of spelling-to-sound unit in a transparent orthography', *The Spanish Journal of Psychology*, 10 (1), 52–67.

Klingberg, T., Forssberg, H. and Westerberg, H. (2002) 'Training of working memory in children with ADHD', *Journal of Clinical and Experimental Neuropsychology*, 24 (6), 781–91.

Klingberg, T., Fernell, E., Olesen, P. J., Johnson, M., Gustafsson, P., Dahlstrom, K., Gillberg, C. G., Forssberg, H. and Westerberg, H. (2005) 'Computerized training of working memory in children with ADHD – a randomized, controlled trial', *Journal of the American Academy of Child and Adolescent Psychiatry*, 44 (2), 177–86.

Knezek, G. and Christensen, R. (2008) 'Effect of technology-based programs on first- and second-grade reading achievement', *Computers in the Schools*, 24 (3 and 4), 23–41.

Ko, M. H. (2005) 'Glosses, comprehension, and strategy use', *Reading in a Foreign Language*, 17 (2), 125–43, available at: http://nflrc.hawaii.edu/rfl/October2005/ko/ko.html

Koul, R., Clariana, R. B. and Salehi, R. (2005) 'Comparing several human and computer-based methods for scoring concept maps and essays', *Journal of Educational Computing Research*, 32 (3), 261–73.

Landauer, T. K., Foltz, P. W. and Laham, D. (1998) 'Introduction to latent semantic analysis', *Discourse Processes*, 25, 259–84, available at: http://lsa.colorado.edu/papers/dp1.LSAintro.pdf

Lange, A. A., McPhillips, M., Mulhern, G. and Wylie, J. (2006) 'Assistive technology tools for secondary-level students with literacy difficulties', *Journal of Special Education Technology*, 21 (3), 13–22.

Licko, Z. and VanderLans, R. (1994) *Émigré: Graphic Design into the Digital Realm*. New York: Wiley.

Lomicka, L. L. (1998) 'To gloss or not to gloss: an investigation of reading comprehension online', *Language Learning & Technology*, 1 (2), 41–50.

Lyytinen, H., Ronimus, M., Alanko, A., Poikkeus, A. and Taanila, M. (2007) 'Early identification of dyslexia and the use of computer game-based practice to support reading acquisition', *Nordic Psychology*, 59 (2), 109–26.

Macaruso, P., Hook, P. E. and McCabe, R. (2006) 'The efficacy of computer-based supplementary phonics programs for advancing reading skills in at-risk elementary students', *Journal of Research of Reading*, 29 (2), 162–72.

Mayer, R. E. and Moreno, R. (1998) 'A split-attention effect in multimedia learning: evidence for dual information processing systems In working memory', *Journal of Educational Psychology*, 90, 312–20.

McLuhan, M. (1964) *Understanding Media: The Extensions of Man*. New York: McGraw-Hill.

McPherson, J. and Burns, N. R. (2008) 'Assessing the validity of computer-game-like tests of processing speed and working memory', *Behavior Research Methods*, 40 (4), 969–81.

Miles, E. (1995) 'Can there be a single definition of dyslexia?', *Dyslexia*, 2 (1), 37–45.

Mitchell, M. J. and Fox, B. J. (2001) 'The effects of computer software for developing phonological awareness in low-progress readers', *Reading Research and Instruction*, 40, 315–32.

Morais, J., Alegria, J. and Content, A. (1987) 'The relationship between segmental analysis and alphabetic literacy', *Cahiers de Psychologie Cognitive*, 7, 415–38.

Moreno, R. and Mayer, R. E. (1999a) 'Cognitive principles of multimedia learning: the role of modality and contiguity', *Journal of Educational Psychology*, 91, 358–68.

— (1999b) 'Visual presentations in multimedia learning: conditions that overload visual working memory', in D. P. Huijsmans and A. W. M. Smeulders (eds) *Lecture Notes in Computer Science: Visual Information and Information Systems* (pp. 793–800). Berlin: Springer Verlag.

Mostow, J., Aist, G., Bey, J., Burkhead, P., Cuneo, A., Junker, B., Rossbach, S., Tobin, B., Valeri, J. and Wilson, S. (2002) Independent practice versus computer-guided oral reading: equal-time comparison of sustained silent reading to an automated reading tutor that listens. Ninth Annual Meeting of the Society for the Scientific Study of Reading, Chicago, IL, 27–30 June.

Nichols, M. (2003) 'A theory for eLearning', *Educational Technology and Society*, 6 (2), 1–10, available at: www.ifets.info/journals/6_2/1.pdf.

Rack, J. P., Hulme, C. and Snowling, M. J. (1993) 'Learning to read: a theoretical synthesis', in H.W. Reeses (ed.) *Advances in Child Development and Behaviour* (Vol. 24). New York: Academic Press.

Raskind, M. H. and Higgins, E. L. (1999) 'Speaking to read: the effects of speech recognition technology on the reading and spelling performance of children with learning disabilities', *Annals of Dyslexia*, 49, 251–81.

Reid, G. (2003) *Dyslexia: A Practitioner's Handbook*. Chichester: Wiley.

Robinson, R. (1950) *Definition*. Oxford: Oxford University Press.

Schofield, J. (2007) 'The PDA is dead, long live the PDA's functions', Guardian Online, available at: www.guardian.co.uk/technology/2007/may/31/comment.guardianweekly technologysection2

Shaikh, A. D. (2005) 'The effects of line length on reading online news', *Usability News,* 7 (2).

Shaikh, A. D., Chaparro, B. S. and Fox, D. (2006) 'Perception of fonts: perceived personality traits and uses', available at: www.surl.org/usabilitynews/81/PersonalityofFonts.asp.

Siegel, L. (1989) 'IQ is irrelevant to the definition of learning disabilities', *Journal of Learning Disabilities*, 22, 469–86.

Siegel, L. and Smythe, I. (2005) 'Reflections on research on reading disability with special attention to gender issues', *Journal of Learning Disabilities*, 5, 473–477.

Singleton, C. H. (2009) Intervention for dyslexia: a review of published evidence on the impact of specialist dyslexia teaching', available at: www.thedyslexia-spldtrust.org.uk/media/downloads/7-intervention-for-dyslexia-research-report.pdf

Singleton, C. and Simmons, F. (2001) 'An evaluation of Wordshark in the classroom', *British Journal of Educational Technology*, 32 (3), 317–30.

Smythe, I. (2004) Dystrain – E-learning dyslexia support training for teachers and parents, available at: www.welshdyslexia.info/dystrain.

— (2006) An international model of reading difficulties. Leonardo Project Include Workshop. Budapest, 2 March.

— (2008) Integrating technology: developing resources for lasting solutions. Early Grade Reading Assessment: Second Workshop, World Bank, 12–14 March, available at: http://siteresources.worldbank.org/EDUCATION/Resources/278200-1121703274255/1439264-1206041771843/ISWBIT.pdf

Smythe, I. and Capellini, S. A (2007) Modelling the role of phonology in the identification of the reading disabled (dyslexic) child, Revista CEFAC, 2007.

Smythe, I. and Everatt, J. (2002) 'Adult dyslexia checklist', in I. Smythe (ed.) *The Dyslexia Handbook*. Reading: British Dyslexia Association.

Snowling, M. J. (2000) *Dyslexia*, 2nd edn. Oxford: Blackwell.

Soe, K., Koki, S. and Chang, J. M. (2000) 'Effect of computer-assisted instruction (CAI) on reading achievement: a meta-analysis', available at: www.prel.org/products/products/Effect-CAI.pdf

Stephens, L. (2000) 'Evaluating the effectiveness of the Touch-Type Read and Spell Computer Aided learning program on two groups of dyslexic children', unpublished BSc thesis in Applied Psychology and Sports Science, Liverpool John Moores University.

Tijms, J. and Hoeks, J. (2005) 'A computerized treatment of dyslexia: benefits from treating lexico-phonological processing problems', *Dyslexia*, 11, 22–40.

Underwood, J. D. M. (2000) 'A comparison of two types of computer support for reading development', *Journal of Research in Reading*, 23 (2), 136–48.

Verezub, E., Grossi, V., Howard, K. and Watkins, P. (2008) 'Building e-based literacy for vocational education and training students', *Australasian Journal of Educational Technology*, 24 (3), 326–38, available at: www.ascilite.org.au/ajet/ajet24/verezub.html.

Whiting, P. R. and Chapman, E. (2000) 'Evaluation of a computer-based program to reach reading and spelling to students with learning difficulties', *Australian Journal of Learning Disabilities*, 5 (4), 11–17.

Wise, B. W., Ring, J. and Olson, R. K. (2000) 'Individual differences in gains from computer-assisted remedial reading', *Journal of Experimental Child Psychology*, 77, 197–205.

Zhu and Smythe, I. (2009) 'Study skills deficits in Chinese students' (submitted).

Index

f or *t* indicate figures or tables

accessibility
  browser settings 134
  e-assessments 28–9, 32
  e-learning 144, 145
  European Union and government
      websites 184
access to privileged information 23, 30
adaptations, computer 28–9
'adopt, adapt, improve' technological
      functions 115–17
assessments
  for adults 18–19
  criterion-referenced testing 15, 16
  diagnostic tests 3, 45
  dyslexia checklists 17–18
  with integrated support 35
  interpreting results 21, 29, 36
  for labelling (dyslexic) 3, 5
  of needs, alternative to labelling 5
  norm-referenced testing 15–17
  as part of learning process 25
for support provision 21–2, 167
  for support technology 13–14, 167
  validity and reliability 24, 25, 26–8
  see also e-assessments
assistive technology
  Disability Discrimination Act 1995 142
  early school years 79
  mobile phones 89
  research 87
  timelines, linear format 89
  visual linear format, transference 88–9
author definition of dyslexia 8, 10
authorship
  coursework 156–8
  homework (multilingualism) 174

background colour and text 130–2,
      132t, 133–4, 136
backup, memory and storage 47, 91–2
Barrington Stoke, publishers, preferred
      format 130, 135
'basic skills', term definition 7–8
Baysian models of learning, cost-
      effectiveness 113
bilingualism
  resources 179
  Wales 172
browsers
  dyslexia-friendly 136–7
  translators 177
browser settings, accessibility 134
Buzan, Tony (mind mapping) 85

Calldysc project *see* Collaborative
      Additional Language Learning for
      Dyslexic
      Schoolchildren project
causes and symptoms
  cognitive difficulties 2, 7
  environmental 2, 3, 4, 17
  neurological 2, 3, 8
  requirement to prove 5
circumstances, effects on difficulties 2,
      3, 4
cognitive difficulties 2, 7, 166–70
cognitive functions, computerised testing
      24, 30
Collaborative Additional Language
      Learning for Dyslexic
      Schoolchildren
      (Calldysc) project 146
  multilingualism 171, 172
  results
      end-user focus groups 147
      teachers integral to e-learning 147
technology goals and timescales 147
      use of technology and support 147

colour blindness 133
computer components
  dual screens, benefits 42–3
  keyboards
    Dvorak 45
    fold-up, benefits 45
    function keys in Word 43
    Maltron 45
    Microsoft Keyboard Layout Creator
      45–6
    Print Screen (Prt Scr) 44
    virtual, difficulties 44
  mice and touchpads 46
    left-handed mice 47
  monitors 40
  processors 39–40
  touch screens, difficulties 41–2
computer operating systems,
      comparisons
  Apple Mac 51
  'The Cloud' 52
  Linux 51
  open source software 51–2
  Windows 51
concept (mind) mapping
  ikon maps 87
  mind maps 85
  software 86–7
  transfer to computer 85
  uses 84, 176
constructed reading programs 111
copyright issues 155, 157–8 see also
      intellectual property rights

data protection 23, 30
data rescue, Print Screen (Prt Scr) 44 see
      also deleted files recovery
Davis website (www.dyslexia.com/info/
      webdesign.htm)
DDA see Disability Discrimination Act
      1995
definition of dyslexia
  author's 8, 10
  Disability Discrimination Act 1995 7
  European Dyslexia Association 2
  mathematical model 10
deleted files recovery 92 see also data
      rescue, Print Screen (Prt Scr)

Department for Education and Skills,
      Higher Education, Working Party
      guidelines 4
designers
  accessible guidelines 184
  and end-users 184
DfES see Department for Education and
      Skills, Higher Education, Working
      party guidelines
diagnosis, definition as a guide 3
diagnostic tests 3, 14–15
'differences', problem terminology 6–7
Dilley, Paul (Central London Assessment
      Services) 32
Disability Discrimination Act 1995
  assistive technology 142
  contraventions, examples 142, 153
  dyslexia definition 7
  laptops 49
disability, dyslexia 7
Disabled Students Allowance 7
drop-down menus 132
DSA see Disabled Students Allowance
dyslexia-friendly
  browsers 136–7
  e-assessments 32
  typeface 122–4, 130
Dystrain, Welsh Dyslexia Project 126t,
      151, 160

early school years, assistive technology
      use 79
e-assessments
  accessibility 28–9
  cognitive functions 24, 30
  dyslexia-friendly 32
  item response (adaptive testing) 22
  standardized instructions 34
  support funding 23
  teaching resource 34–5
  tools
    informed choice 20, 22, 23
    key types 19
    levels of feedback required 21, 22,
      23
    purposes 21, 22, 23
  validity and reliability 24, 25, 26–8
EDA see European Dyslexia Association

educational psychologists 3–4, 5
Edysgate, European Union (Grundtvig) – funded project 105
e-learning
  asynchronous
    accessibility 150–51
    advantages 150
    support 151
  for the individual
    benefits to all 144
    developers and end-users 145
    educational accessibility 145
    flexible approaches 143
    how content delivered 148
    information accessibility 144
    knowledge retrieval 148
    learning tools 144
    online / offline advances 145
    potential 145
    technology development and use 143
  support forms
    chat and conferencing 153–4
    email and software 152
    forums (mis)use 153
    (micro)blogging 154
    shared environments 155
  synchronous
    components 149–50
    importance of lecturer / teacher 150
    software 149
Emime project, spoken language translator 174
end-users
  and designers 184–5
  preferences, tips 136
EPs *see* educational psychologists
European Dyslexia Association
  dyslexia definition 2
  effects on funding 7
  skills affected 2
European Union and government websites, accessibility 184
examination marking, computerized
  concept mapping 162–3
  cost-effectiveness 159
  multiple choice questions 160
  open essays 161
  short-text answers 160–61

examinations taken on computers
  multiple choice questions 160
  Norwegian example 158

familiarity, relevance of 28–9, 122, *126t*, 130
fonts 120, 123–6, *126t*, 130, 134, 135
funding support
  definition as a guide 3–4, 5, 7
  e-assessments 23

Geske (www. public.iastate.edu/~geske/ scholarship.html) 124
glossing (annotation) technique 111
grammar checking and spellchecking 89–90
grammar, syntax and punctuation skills, acquisition 112

Heisenberg's Uncertainty Principle 34
Hillier, Rob (*www.robsfonts.com/ sylexiadserif.html*) 123

ICE(D) *see* 'In Case of Emergency Dyslexia' list
'In Case of Emergency Dyslexia' list 93
Institute of Education Sciences, US Department of Education, efficacy reports 111–12
IQ testing, irrelevance *see* intelligence quotient testing, irrelevance
instructions in e-assessments 34
integrated testing and support 35
intellectual property rights 25, 59, 157–8
  see also copyright issues
intelligence quotient testing, irrelevance 3
IPR *see* intellectual property rights
item response (adaptive testing) 22

Kindle, Amazon's e-book 137

labelling (dyslexic)
  reasons against 7, 36
  reasons for 5
laptops 48, 49, 51
law suits, equal opportunity and accessibility issues 137

layout issues
    background colour and text 130–32, *132t*, 133–4, 136
    Barrington – Stoke, publishers, format 130, 135
    drop-down menus 132
    line length and columns 134
    scrolled or paged content 135
    white space 135
literacy skills, acquisition process 99–100

magnifiers on-screen, software 95–6
mapping (technology)
    the reading process 68, *68f*
    the writing process 69, *69f*
matching technology to the individual 97–8, 108, 131, 139, 142
mathematical model, to form dyslexia definition 10
metacognitive strategies, teaching 111
Microsoft Word AutoSummarize, testing 83
mind mapping *see* concept mapping
mobile phones 59–62, 177
    Collaborative Additional Language Learning for Dyslexic Schoolchildren 146
    concept mapping 89
    speech-to-text 78
    translation tools 180
    where am I? 64
Mulcahy, Patrick, (Consultant ETAT (SE) Ltd) 32
multilingualism and dyslexia
    assistive software requirements 173–4
    auditory processing and assessment 166–7
    authorship of homework 174
    cognitive difficulties 166–70
    Emime project 174
    lexical skills and software 170
    motor skills and software 167–70
    orthographic processing and software 169
    speech/sound synthesis and software 168–9
    supportive technology
      concept mapping 176

supportive technology *(cont.)*
    mobile phones 177
    speech-to-text 175–6
    spellcheckers and grammar checkers 176
    text-to-speech 175
    typing 176
support required 182
technology as a motivator 172–3
translation software
    browser 177
    built-in web page 178
    commercial 180
    desktop widgets 178
    Emime project 174
    free online 178
    handheld 180
    hovering 179
    mobile phones 180
    speech-to-speech 180
    tools 180
    types 171
    visual processing and software 169
multilingualism, online resources, non-dyslexic 181
multimedia learning 106–7

navigational development issues 118
needs, assessment of, alternative to labelling 5
needs, identification of specific 36
neurological causes 2, 3, 8
note taking and recording software 95
Novak, Joseph, Cornell University 84, 85

Ogden, Charles, 850 Basic English words (*http://ogden.basic-english.org/*) 167
operating systems, comparisons *see* computer operating systems, comparisons

password recall assistance 92–3
phonological skills 107–9
plagiarism
    accidental 157
    detection software 157–8
predictive software 91

pressure groups 7
Print Screen (Prt Scr), as data rescue 44
privileged information, access to 23, 30
promotion of existing legislation 185
proofreading 90
public awareness requirement 185

Quality Marks, awards 185
quality, websites 185

reading comprehension 109–10
recovery of deleted files 92
reliability of assessments 24, 25, 26–8
reminders, desktop and email 93–4
research, efficacy reports 111–12
research findings
   assistive technology 87
   background colour and text *132t*
   constructed reading programs 111
   fonts and sizes 124–6
   glossing (annotation) technique 111
   line length and columns 134
   literacy development software 104–5
   memory software 103–4
   metacognitive strategies teaching 111
   multimedia learning 106–7
   phonological skills teaching 107–9
   reading comprehension software
      109–10
   scrolled or paged content 135
   speech-to-text 110
   supportive technology 106
   tools, benefits 95
   white space, use 135
research, potential for bias 111–12
research, progression and non-
      achievement 113
research requirements 163
results, interpretation 21, 29, 36
retesting, as part of learning process 24,
      25, 26–8

satnavs 82
scrolled or paged content 135
skills affected
   diversity 9
   European Dyslexia Association 2
skills development, way forward in
      support 36

skill testing, irrelevance in diagnostic
      assessment 3
software
   e-learning 149, 152, 154
   free versus commercial 74–5
   lexical skills 170
   literacy development 104–5
   magnifiers, on-screen 95–6
   memory 103–4
   motor skills 167–70
   multimedia learning 107
   note taking and recording 95
   orthographic processing 169
   phonological skills 108
   plagiarism detection 157–8
   predictive 91
   to provide learning process 100–102
   reading comprehension 109–10
   screen recording 95
   screensharing 96
   shared document 96
   sound recording 95
   speech / sound synthesis
   synthesizing and summarizing 82–3
   time management 94
   video conferencing 96
   visual processing 169
software designers and authors, tips 119
software designers, technologists versus
      educationalists 141
software requirements, multilingualism
      support 173–4
speech-to-text
   description 78
   microphone quality 78–9, 95
   mobile phone services 78
   multilingualism 175–6, 177–80
   recording other voices 79, 95
   research findings 110
spellchecking and grammar checking
      89–90, 176
standardization of definition, reasons
      3–4
study skills 31
support
   assessments as a guide 21–2
   funding
      definition as a guide 3–4, 5, 7
      e-assessments 23

importance of technology 37–8
and integrated testing 35
skills development 36
by teacher 147,150, 151, 166
supportive technology 106
multilingualism 175–6, 177–80
see also technological support devices
symptoms and causes 6
environmental 2, 3, 4, 17
neurological 2, 3, 8
requirement to prove 5
syntax, grammar and punctuation,
acquisition of skills 112

teacher support 147, 150, 151, 166
teaching resources, computerized testing
34–5
technological development issues 117–
18
technological functions, 'adopt, adapt,
improve' 115–17
technological progress and diversity 37,
38–9, 65
technological support, devices
calculator, talking 63
directional GPS guide, problems 64
hand-held spellcheckers and
thesauruses 54–5
headphones 63–4
mobile phones 59–62, 64
note-taking pens 63
Personal Digital Assistant (PDA) 54, 62
satnavs 82
scanners and optical character
recognition (OCR) 55–9
sound recording 52–3
see also supportive technology
technology, assistive see assistive
technology
technology, benefits 185–9
technology selection model 33
technology as support 37–8
assessment 13–14
ten-point plan for the future 184–5
testing see assessments
text-to-speech (TTS)
blog readers 75
classic (toolbar type) 72

text-to-speech (TTS) (cont.)
developments in parameters 77
embedded talking tools
Adobe Read OutLoud 74
webpage based 73–4
file uploading 75
mobile phones 75
online cut and paste 73
outputs, live and recorded 76
principles 71
proofreading 90
quality testing 76–7
stand-alone cut and paste 72
talking web browsers 73
talking word processors 73
uses 70–1, 175
website readers 75
see also speech-to-text
time management software 94
tips for software designers and authors
119
tools see e-assessment tools
training, requirements and provision
96–7
translators see multilingualism,
translation software
typing
auto correction 81–2
discussion 80–1
multilingualism 176
Wordshark 109
typographical issues
summary 119–20
typeface
British Dyslexia Association
publications 121
dyslexia-friendly suggestions 122–4,
130
familiarity preference 122, 126t,
130
fonts 120, 124–6, 126t, 130
kerning and ligature, space between
letters 127, 130
justification 129, 130
leading, line spacing 128, 130, 135
legibility 127

user groups, importance of engaging
184–5

user preferences, tips 136

validity, assessments 24, 25, 26–8
video conferencing software 96
Vinegrad, Michael, dyslexia checklists
    online version (*www.amidyslexic.co.uk/*
      am-i-dyslexic.html) 17
    paper version, Educare, 1994 17–18

visual stress 31

websites, quality 185
white space, use 135
Wordshark 109
work assessments 18–19
work skills 31
writing frames, usefulness 112

Dyslexia is a complex condition, and every dyslexic needs a different solution. Technology is not that solution, but a part of the process to minimise the impact of dyslexia on individuals and to assist with the difficulties they face in everyday situations, so that they can demonstrate their potential in school or at work.

This book takes the reader back to basics, from understanding the needs of the dyslexic individual to getting the most from available technology. It does this by providing frameworks from theoretical perspectives and following this through to practical implementation, including reviews of the most common types of software. There is plenty of practical advice on how to support dyslexic individuals using technology, including how to get the most out of what is available. It highlights state of the art technology, and suggests what more still needs to be done to make this technology truly enabling for all dyslexics.

Dr Ian Smythe is an international dyslexia consultant who lectures widely on using technology to support dyslexic individuals. He has developed a series of EU funded projects, including e-learning for teachers, pan-European assistive technology surveys, training for lecturers and managers, using technology for cognitive development, self-identification and support for dyslexic adults and language learning on mobile phones.